Stefan Buczacki

Best Evergreen Trees and Shrubs

HAMLYN

Publishing Director Laura Bamford
Creative Director Keith Martin
Executive Editor Julian Brown
Design Manager Bryan Dunn
Designer TT Designs
Editor Karen O'Grady
Production Controller Clare Smedley
Picture Research Sally Claxton
Researcher Liz Dobbs
Special Photography Howard Rice

First published in Great Britain in 1999
by Hamlyn, an imprint of
Octopus Publishing Group Limited
2-4 Heron Quays, London, E14 4JP

Produced by Toppan
Printed in Hong Kong

A catalogue record for this book is available from
the British Library

ISBN 0600 596737

CONTENTS

INTRODUCTION 4

WHAT ARE CONIFERS? 6

CONIFERS AND EVERGREENS IN THE GARDEN 8

PLANTING AND AFTER-CARE 12

SHRUBS 14

CONIFERS 72

NON-CONIFEROUS TREES 86

INDEX 94

INTRODUCTION

Thank goodness for evergreens. Yes, of course there are winter-flowering plants and some winter-flowering bulbs. Without evergreen shrubs and trees, however, the garden in winter would be a fairly bleak place. This much is undeniable, but it is all too common an error to consider evergreens only in terms of their role in the garden in winter. Perhaps that is when they are at their most obvious but it is very far from the only time that they are important. The point I want to emphasise is that the contribution evergreen plants make to the overall framework and structure of the garden for the entire year is all too frequently overlooked.

Evergreens complement deciduous plants by virtue very often of their different leaf shape and texture and, especially with conifers, of their rather different overall form. But just why the essential difference between deciduous plants and evergreens arose is almost anyone's guess because botany hasn't produced a really satisfactory explanation. When fossil plants are studied, it is found that the earliest types were all evergreen and that the deciduous habit evolved relatively late in geological time. The best explanation seems to be that it was a complicated response to moderate but not severe seasonal cold, high summer humidity and other factors.

In reality, the term 'evergreen' refers to the plant not to the foliage for evergreens don't retain their leaves permanently; they simply shed them piecemeal throughout the year instead of in one fell swoop every autumn. Anyone who has tried weeding under a holly will testify to the fact that the leaves do drop. There are indeed many genera, and some of them very important garden plant groups like *Magnolia*, *Berberis* and *Lonicera*, that contain both deciduous and evergreen species, although in most groups, one system predominates. There is, for instance, only one significant evergreen magnolia in the shape of *Magnolia grandiflora* while there are well 100 deciduous forms. Almost all conifers are evergreen although the larches are among the few notable exceptions.

Ecologically, the evergreen habit has some important consequences: in a

Cotoneaster dammeri

ABOVE: *Laurus nobilis*

LEFT: *Ceanothus arboreus* **'Trewithen Blue'**

selected what I consider to be the best types for garden use and have arranged them in three main groupings: conifers, other evergreen trees and evergreen shrubs. For each main entry, I have described special features of the foliage (after all, by no means all evergreens have green leaves) and also any flowering or fruiting appeal that increases their garden value.

As evergreen shrubs and trees are often used as hedging plants, I have indicated those that I find particularly good for this purpose. And, as with other books in the series, I have shown which of my recommended varieties have been awarded the AGM (Award of Garden Merit) by the Royal Horticultural Society. This is a useful indicator of plants that, in independent trials, have proved their worth as garden plants although it doesn't, of course, guarantee that you will necessarily like them.

mixed vegetation community, whether in a garden or in the wild, an evergreen species will cast shade all year round with major consequences for any plant trying to grow beneath. It will also have the effect of rendering that species more liable to the effects of winter wind or snow damage, because it presents a large surface area against which

strong winds can blow or on which snow can accumulate. But, conversely, it gives the plant a 'head start' with growth in the spring, since there's no need to wait for buds to open before photosynthesis can begin.

The fact is that conifers and other evergreens are now very important garden plants. In this book, I have

WHAT ARE CONIFERS?

These plants have become hugely familiar in all our gardens, the word trips off the tongue as readily as daisy or dandelion, and we have one example in our homes, decorated and illuminated, every Christmas. But when put on the spot and asked to define exactly what it is about a conifer that makes it different from other types of garden tree, many gardeners would be somewhat hesitant.

The biggest clue lies in that name, conifer, meaning a plant bearing cones. There are very few other types of seed-bearing plants with cones, and certainly none in most gardens. Cone-like fruits on such plants as the ornamental hop are quite different and the resemblance is fortuitous. Rather confusingly, however, in conifers, the cones assume the role both of the flowers and the fruits of flowering plants. Among common species, this is best seen in the larch. The bright red, superficially flower-like structures on the twigs in the spring are immature cones. The females subsequently progress to form the more typical dry mature seed-bearing cones later in life.

The mature cone of a conifer displays moreover one very important difference from the fruits of flowering seed plants. On a cone, the seeds are exposed throughout their development and you will readily see them between the hardy woody scales, from where they fall out when mature. In a fruit, the seeds are enclosed and the fruit itself must split open in some way to liberate them.

As always in life, there are a few exceptions to these generalisations and in gardens, the most important is the yew, an immensely valuable and beautiful tree. Although generally classified with the other conifers, it doesn't bear cones; its seeds are borne singly, wrapped in a red fleshy structure called an aril.

Conifers are hugely important plants; coniferous forests cover vast areas of the earth's surface and both the tallest and oldest living things are species of coniferous tree. The feature that brings them appropriately into this book, however, is the fact that most are evergreen. Again, there are a few exceptions (the larch, swamp cypress and the dawn redwood are the commonest) but the others have evergreen foliage that has developed a distinctly reduced form. Conifer foliage appears either as needles (as in pines and

Pinus wallichiana

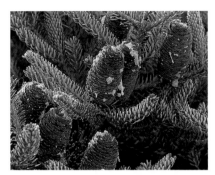

ABOVE: *Abies koreana* **'Silberlocke'**

RIGHT: *Taxus baccata* **'Standishii'**

spruces) or as small flattened scale leaves (as in cypresses). These are both adaptations in keeping with the cold climates in which most conifers live. All conifer leaves have a small surface area in relation to their volume and a thick, waxy cuticle or skin, both of which cut down water loss. At first sight, this seems incongruous; eliminating water loss might be thought of importance only for plants of deserts and other dry places. But in reality, the fact that the soil is frozen for long periods in cold regions means that plants are unable to take up water to replace any lost through the leaves, so cutting down water loss is very important. The waxy, slippery surface of the foliage, combined in many instances with a pyramidal overall shape to the plants (think of the Christmas tree) is believed to be an adaptation to facilitate snow sliding off the branches.

The fact that conifers are trees, not shrubs, might be thought to limit their value as ornamentals, but not a bit of it. No other group of garden trees is so blessed with dwarf, shrub-sized varieties that find homes in gardens both large and small.

CONIFERS AND EVERGREENS IN THE GARDEN

Evergreen plants can be grouped into categories, depending on the relative importance of the evergreen habit:

• The plant has no flowers (a conifer) although it might have interesting and attractive cones;

• The plant has flowers of little interest but does have uniformly green and fairly interestingly shaped foliage;

• The plant has flowers of little interest but does have interestingly coloured (generally variegated) foliage;

• The plant has evergreen foliage of some form but its attractiveness really lies in its flowers.

These clearly dictate some of the ways in which they will be most successful in gardens but, above all, it is as a garden backcloth, a carpet, that green-leaved evergreens have their greatest value. It is against their foliage that flowers and other leaf colours are shown off to best advantage; and as almost all other plants possess green colouration to some degree, they very seldom cause disharmony or strident clashes. Put quite simply, they blend with almost everything but the following are my suggestions of some of the ways in which you might like to consider using them.

In containers

Evergreens make fairly good container plants although, among conifers, only the dwarf varieties are successful, mainly because they are prone to damage from drying out and because the hot, dry conditions that often prevail in containers are very conducive to red spider mite attack. In addition, damage can occur in small containers that freeze in winter, giving rise to the water shortage problems that I referred to on page 7.

Mahonia x *media* '**Lionel Fortescue**'

Ruta graveolens 'Jackman's Blue'

Beds of evergreens

All-evergreen beds of low-growing shrubs (those popularly called ground-cover shrubs) offer an excellent solution to the planting of difficult areas, and can sometimes be attractive even in places that wouldn't be considered difficult. But it is a type of planting that can be over-done and is too often used as an easy option when a mixed or otherwise more imaginative scheme would be better.

Variegated evergreens

Variegated foliage, whether evergreen or deciduous, is both a blessing and a curse. The variegation can take many forms and when used in combination with all-green leaves, almost invariably looks attractive. But as a backdrop to flowers, it can be confusing to the eye and the one can easily minimise, rather than enhance, the effects of the other.

Evergreens with bulbs

Evergreen trees and shrubs can be very attractive in combination with bulbs but only if the plantings are done with care. Early blooming bulbs are effective beneath deciduous shrubs as they flower before the leaves emerge and the canopy closes above them. Evergreens however cast shade all year round and bulbs planted beneath them won't therefore be successful. Always position bulbs in front of any evergreen plantings therefore. And don't plant bulbs very close to conifers; the shallow mat of fibrous roots will almost always impede their satisfactory establishment.

Evergreens in mixed borders

I feel that evergreen shrubs probably have their greatest garden value in providing the permanent framework to mixed borders (those borders where herbaceous perennials and shrubs are inter-planted). They offer the winter interest that is so important after the herbaceous perennials have died down and provide an interesting contrast to the bare stems of deciduous types.

Hebe cupressoides **'Boughton Dome'**

Shrubberies

Originally, the garden shrubbery was very largely a planting of evergreens. And in the 19th century, a sombre mixture of plants such as holly, laurel and privet typically surrounded many a country house. Today, a blend of deciduous and evergreen species is considered much more attractive, but their relative positioning is important. If your requirement is at least partly for screening, do be sure that the evergreens are in the most critical places; you can see through a deciduous shrub in winter.

Beneath trees

Growing anything in deep shade is difficult; growing anything beneath evergreen trees is doubly so; growing anything beneath yew is rather like trying to garden at night. Because evergreen shrubs have foliage all year round, they need light all year round too, so in winter, when light levels are at their lowest, an evergreen shrub beneath an evergreen tree is bound to find life difficult. Very, very few will come near to tolerating these conditions, as will be evident from my book *Best Shade Plants*.

The conifer garden

Although conifers have been grown in gardens almost as long as people have gardened, the development and discovery of large numbers of dwarf varieties over the past 40 or so years has given rise to a highly individual garden style. The conifer garden (or as it often tended to be, the conifer and heather garden) probably reached its zenith in the 1970s, when it divided gardening opinion sharply. People either loved it or hated it although, even then, I think there was general recognition that it only really looked right adjoining a modern house. Today, even the strongest adherents of this garden style tend to soften the appearance and enhance the variety by including some herbaceous perennials, ornamental grasses, bulbs and other plants too.

Ilex x altaclarensis **'Golden King'**

PLANTING AND AFTER-CARE

Planting

The planting of evergreens is little different from the planting of any other tree or shrub but there are a few special considerations. Your plants will probably be bought in containers of potting compost; and even mail-order plants are likely to be sent in this way. It's unlikely that evergreens will be delivered bare-rooted, as many deciduous plants are, for the very reason that they do have foliage all year round and are, therefore, constantly losing moisture through their leaves. And again, for the same reason, moving evergreens is an operation to be undertaken with great care. It should always be done in the dormant season when the weather is mild, and the plants must be watered in very thoroughly afterwards, as their roots must never be allowed to dry out. Conifers especially are difficult to transplant successfully because they have a shallow mass of fibrous roots and a huge foliage area; and large conifers, even grown in containers, establish less readily than other large evergreens.

When planting a container-grown evergreen, prepare a planting position by digging a hole of roughly twice the volume of the pot-ball of compost. The soil removed should be mixed with an approximately equal volume of compost or similar organic matter plus a few handfuls of bone meal. Very gently tease away the roots from the edge of the compost ball and then firm the soil carefully with your boot as you fill the hole. Finish by making a small mound with the soil sloping downwards away from the plant's stem to prevent water collecting at the base and freezing. If you are planting evergreens in autumn, and especially if you live in a cold or exposed area, it's wise to erect a temporary screen of hessian or similar material to keep off the worst effects of the winter wind.

Food and water

As I have indicated, adequate water is especially important for evergreens, and most especially in the early stages. But they will also benefit from the continued addition of an organic mulch to the soil in the spring while the ground is still moist. Garden compost is an ideal mulch for most types of evergreen, although for those such as rhododendrons or camellias that require acidic conditions, conifer needles are also excellent.

Like all other plants, conifers and evergreens will benefit from an

Pyracantha coccinea 'Orange Glow'

application of fertiliser, also in spring. Although a general shrub or rose fertiliser will give good results, it is worth trying to be a bit more precise by taking account of the needs of the plant. If you have chosen it primarily for its flowers, then rose fertiliser, relatively high in flower-promoting potash, is the best. If the plant is essentially a foliage choice (and this applies to all conifers, of course, and most hedges), then select a fertiliser such as blood, fish and bone that has relatively more leaf-promoting nitrogen.

Pests and diseases

All plants suffer to some extent from pests and diseases. The presence of foliage all year round on evergreens however confers some particular complications. Whilst most diseases are in a relatively dormant state in the winter, some pests, both large and small, are active and evergreens offer a ready supply of green food. In mild winters especially therefore, you can expect some damage from slugs, vine weevils and other leaf eating creatures. If you wish to use an insecticide to control them, be aware of two things. First, that some pesticides are much less effective in cooler weather and results may not be as good as in the summer. And second, that one of the most useful pesticides that is intended for routine winter application, a spray called tar oil which is used to kill pests hiding among the bark, cannot be used on any evergreen plants because it damages green tissue. I have given extensive information on the identification and treatment of pests and diseases in my book *Best Garden Doctor*.

Conifers tend to be affected by a rather different range of pests and diseases from other evergreen shrubs and trees. Again, further information is given in *Best Garden Doctor* but one symptom especially is very common and very difficult to diagnose. Browning of the foliage on conifers can arise from a wide variety of reasons. Among the commoner possibilities are: root rot or other root damage, winter cold, salt (when trees or hedges are adjacent to roads on which de-icing salt has been used), red spider mite, aphids, adelgids (aphid-like creatures peculiar to conifers) and honey fungus.

Itea ilicifolia

SHRUBS

Acacia dealbata AGM Silver wattle

I often feel that, wonderful as the climate of western Europe is for gardening, its hard winters mean that we are blissfully unaware of some of the most important groups of plants on a global scale. And there's hardly any better example of this than the genus Acacia, a huge group of over 1200 species belonging to the pea family. Gardeners in warm climates and in the southern hemisphere especially know many of them as wattles, but unfamiliar though they may be, northern gardeners with a mild and sheltered spot will find at least one of the species to be richly rewarding.

Acacia dealbata

FLOWERING or FRUITING INTEREST: The fragrant golden yellow flowers are the fluffy 'mimosa' valued by flower arrangers. Flowers appear in late winter in the mildest areas or early spring.

FOLIAGE INTEREST: Fern-like leaves of silver-green.

SUITABILITY AS HEDGING: None in the British climate but could be used as a windbreak in frost-free areas.

SITE AND SOIL: Originates from south-east Australia so in Britain needs a sheltered site with abundant sun. A sunny, sheltered wall and a light, well-drained soil are ideal but in mild areas it can be grown as a free-standing specimen. In colder districts it may be grown in a container as a conservatory plant.

HARDINESS: Barely hardy to fairly hardy; one of the hardiest acacias.

SPECIAL CARE: No pruning necessary. A hard winter can cause damage which should be cut out after flowering, cutting at least 30cm (1ft) into undamaged wood. This species produces suckers, an indication that it can regenerate from the base. Propagate by semi-ripe cuttings in summer.

SIZE: A fast- growing plant capable of attaining 8m (25ft) in five years but in a climate such as that of Britain 6-10 x 4-6m (20-33 x 13-20ft) after 10 years is more typical.

SIGNIFICANT PROBLEMS

May be damaged by hard winters and can become chlorotic on alkaline soils.

> **Recommended Varieties**
> The normal species only is available.

Andromeda polifolia Bog rosemary

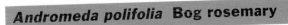

FLOWERING or FRUITING INTEREST: Small hanging bell-like flowers of soft pink appear from late spring to early summer.

FOLIAGE INTEREST: The slender stems bear narrow glaucous-green leaves with white downy undersides.

SUITABILITY AS HEDGING: None.

SITE AND SOIL: Must have a damp acidic soil; light shade is preferred and if growing in a sunny position, ensure that the soil retains moisture over the summer. May also be grown satisfactorily in a container with lime-free compost.

HARDINESS: Barely hardy to fairly hardy.

SPECIAL CARE: Provided the soil is suitable, needs little special care, no pruning is necessary and it suffers few problems. May be propagated by softwood cuttings taken in late summer.

SIZE: A dwarf shrub attaining only.

Andromeda polifolia 'Alba'

60 x 60cm (2 x 2ft) after five years and never attaining more than 1 x 1.2-1.5m (3 x 4-5ft).

SIGNIFICANT PROBLEMS
None.

Arctostaphylos uva-ursi
Red bearberry

FLOWERING or FRUITING INTEREST: In late spring or early summer, white-tinged pink flowers hang like small bells over the plant. Small spherical red fruits are produced in autumn.

FOLIAGE INTEREST: Small bright green leaves with some red markings on stems.

SUITABILITY AS HEDGING: None.

SITE AND SOIL: An acidic soil in full sun is essential; it is intolerant of alkalinity, shade or water-logging. Use it as a low creeping shrub in an acidic garden soil or allow it to colonise a sandy bank where it will tolerate the dry and poor conditions.

HARDINESS: Hardy.

SPECIAL CARE: Apart from its precise site and soil conditions, needs little attention. No pruning or special feeding are necessary. When mulching, it is best to use an acidic mulch such as chopped conifer needles. To propagate, take softwood cuttings in summer or lift self-rooted layers from the parent plant.

SIZE: Maintains its dwarf height of 50cm (1¾ft) but spreads from 60cm (2ft) after five years to form a 1m (3ft) mat after 20 years.

SIGNIFICANT PROBLEMS
None.

Arctostaphylos uva-ursi
'Vancouver Jade'

Aucuba japonica Spotted laurel

" *No shrub that I have ever grown is more tolerant of shady, dry places than this one. In my own garden, it even grows beneath a beech tree and provided it isn't totally neglected when the water and fertiliser are being dispensed,* Aucuba *will seldom let you down.* "

FLOWERING or FRUITING INTEREST: Female forms have spherical, usually red fruits.

FOLIAGE INTEREST: The species has bright all-green oval leaves but its varieties are often splashed with cream or yellow markings.

SUITABILITY AS HEDGING: Moderately effective as fillers for shaded parts of a mixed hedge.

SITE AND SOIL: Tolerates shade, pollution and extremes of soil conditions. Some pale-leaved forms can scorch in hot sun.

HARDINESS: Very hardy.

SPECIAL CARE: None, but for fruits, plant a female and a male form (such as the species). No pruning necessary. To propagate, take softwood cuttings in early summer or hardwood cuttings in a cold frame in autumn/winter.

SIZE: 1 x 1m (3 x 3ft) in the early years but ultimately 4 x 3.5m (13 x 11ft).

SIGNIFICANT PROBLEMS

None; the shoot tips sometimes blacken and I suspect *Botrytis*.

Recommended Varieties

Varieties of *A. japonica*: leaves with masses of small yellow spots; 'Golden King', male, otherwise similar to 'Crotonifolia'; 'Longifolia' AGM, female with elongated bright green leaves; 'Salicifolia', female, abundant fruits, narrow plain green leaves; 'Variegata' (syn. 'Maculata'), female, irregular cream leaf spots.

Aucuba japonica **'Longifolia'**

Berberis Barberry

FLOWERING or FRUITING INTEREST: Yellow or orange flowers in spring or early summer, often followed by dark blue fruits.

FOLIAGE INTEREST: Generally small, oval to elongated leaves in varying shades of green, some (even evergreen varieties) offer autumn colour.

SUITABILITY AS HEDGING: Good, used as informal flowering hedges. Spiny forms will help to deter intruders.

SITE AND SOIL: A fairly sheltered site in light shade or sun. *Berberis* will thrive in most garden soils except very dry sites.

HARDINESS: Hardy to very hardy, but a few like *B. x lologensis* and *B. linearifolia* are more tender.

SPECIAL CARE: None; pruning not necessary. To propagate, take softwood cuttings in early summer or semi-ripe cuttings in early autumn.

Berberis x stenophylla **'Claret Cascade'**

SIZE: Varies with species but most are between 1.2 x 1.2m (4 x 4ft) and 1.5 x 1.5m (5 x 5ft) when mature.

SIGNIFICANT PROBLEMS
None.

Recommended Varieties
B. buxifolia 'Pygmaea' (syn. 'Nana'), low, spreading, pale green leaves, small spines, double yellow flowers. *B. darwinii* AGM, medium/tall, small leaves, spiny, vivid orange flowers, a glorious plant, 'the finest evergreen ever to be grown in a British garden'. *B. x frikartii* 'Amstelveen' AGM, fast growing with arching branches, glossy green leaves with blue-white undersides. *B. gagnepainii* var. *lanceifolia*, tall, holly-like leaves, good for boundary planting as it spreads by suckering. *B. julianae*, tall, dull green leaves with some autumn colour, long thorns, large pale yellow flowers. *B. linearifolia* 'Orange King', tall, mid-green narrow leaves with silver undersides, spiny, vivid orange flowers. *B. x lologensis* 'Apricot Queen' AGM, upright habit, large bright orange flowers, spiny. *B. x stenophylla* AGM, tall, olive-green leaves with silver undersides, long thorns, masses of yellow flowers in spring; *B. x s.* 'Claret Cascade', smaller than the normal hybrid, red-purple stems, red buds, orange flowers; *B. x s.* 'Corallina Compacta' AGM, dwarf form, only 30cm (1ft) high, coral-pink buds, yellow flowers. *B. x verruculosa* AGM, low growing, spreading habit, oval leaves of olive-green with silver undersides, spines, semi-double yellow flowers.

Brachyglottis (syn. *Senecio*) Shrubby ragwort

FLOWERING or FRUITING INTEREST: Yellow or white daisy-like flowers in early to midsummer.

FOLIAGE INTEREST: Silver-grey foliage, often with a woolly appearance.

SUITABILITY AS HEDGING: None as a barrier but can be grown as low hedge and useful in a coastal garden.

SITE AND SOIL: Always best in full sun. Tolerates drought and wind (if not cold); ideal for coastal gardens. It thrives in most soils but not on heavy clay or water-logged sites.

HARDINESS: Varies; some, like *B.* 'Sunshine' and *B. monroi* are moderately hardy to hardy, others like *B.* 'Moira Reid' are only barely hardy to fairly hardy.

SPECIAL CARE NEEDED: Very little. Trim back lightly with shears after flowering; old, lax plants should be cut back hard in spring. To propagate either take semi-ripe cuttings in summer or hardwood cuttings in autumn.

SIZE: Will reach a maximum of 1-1.5m x 1-1.5m (3-5 x 3-5ft) within five years.

SIGNIFICANT PROBLEMS
Aphids and fungal leaf spots.

Recommended Varieties
B. 'Moira Reid' (syn. 'Sunshine Variegated'), white hairy leaves that age to dark green with yellow variegation. *B.* 'Sunshine' (syns. *Senecio greyi*, *S.* 'Sunshine') AGM , silver to grey-green leaves with white felted undersides, yellow flowers. *B. monroi* (syn. *Senecio monroi*) AGM, dark grey leaves with wavy edges, young shoots grey to white, yellow daisy flowers, smaller denser shrub than 'Sunshine'.

Brachyglottis monroi

17

Buxus sempervirens AGM Box

❝ Box is one of the great shrubs of British and European history. In times past, fairly extensive pure stands existed naturally and its fine-grained wood was prized for turning. As a garden plant, it played an invaluable role when formal gardening was at its peak for few other plants are so attractively appropriate for hedges, tall and short. The interest in formal planting on a small scale today has seen renewed interest; and sadly, elevated prices for plants at nurseries and garden centres. ❞

FLOWERING or FRUITING INTEREST: None.

FOLIAGE INTEREST: Small glossy dark green leaves, some forms are variegated.

SUITABILITY AS HEDGING: Excellent, especially for low hedges.

SITE AND SOIL: Very tolerant of most conditions including alkalinity. Tolerates deep shade although variegated forms benefit from sun.

HARDINESS: Very hardy.

SPECIAL CARE: None is essential but it is often clipped to shape and makes a good topiary subject. Clip in midsummer and then again in mid autumn. Can be pruned back hard in late spring if necessary although doesn't regenerate from very old wood as effectively as yew.

To propagate, take semi-ripe cuttings in summer or hardwood cuttings in autumn.

SIZE: The more vigorous forms will attain 5-6m (16-20ft) in height and spread if left unclipped but in practice most are clipped to much less; dwarf box hedging may readily be kept to 15-30cm (6in-1ft) high.

SIGNIFICANT PROBLEMS

Box aphids, whiteflies, box sucker.

Recommended Varieties

B. microphylla 'Faulkner', upright, small fresh green leaves. *B. s.* 'Aureovariegata' (syn. 'Aurea'), rounded leaves with golden edges and some gold blotches; *B. s.* 'Elegantissima' (syn. 'Silver Variegated') AGM, small irregularly-shaped leaves with white edges, slow growing, often reverts to green if clipped; *B. s.* 'Marginata' (syn. *B. s.* 'Aureo Marginata'), yellow margins on dark green leaves; *B. s.* 'Suffruticosa' AGM, small leaves, very slow growing, ideal as dwarf edging.

Buxus sempervirens **'Aureovariegata'**

Callistemon citrinus Bottle brush

FLOWERING or FRUITING INTEREST: Red flowers of an unusual bottle brush shape appear in summer.

FOLIAGE INTEREST: Narrow rigid leaves, rather reminiscent of rosemary, that emit a lemon scent when crushed.

SUITABILITY AS HEDGING: None.

SITE AND SOIL: *C. citrinus* is hardy enough to grow outdoors, at least in sheltered gardens although not on shallow alkaline soils.

HARDINESS: Barely to fairly hardy.

SPECIAL CARE: Old specimens will benefit from having one or two of the oldest shoots removed periodically.

To propagate, raise from seed or take softwood cuttings in late spring or early summer.

SIZE: A fast growing plant attaining 3 x 2.4m (10 x 6¾ft) in 10 years.

SIGNIFICANT PROBLEMS

None.

Callistemon citrinus **'Splendens'**

Recommended Varieties
Several species are available from specialists but *C. citrinus* is the most widely found. *C. c.* 'Splendens' AGM at 1.8m (5¾ft) is not as large as the true species and has showier flowers of a more brilliant red.

Calluna vulgaris Heather

FLOWERING or FRUITING INTEREST: Most have masses of small summer flowers in shades of mauve, red, pink or white although they are individually less spectacular than those of Erica.
FOLIAGE INTEREST: Tiny leaves that *en masse* give a feathery appearance, leaf colour changes through the seasons.
SUITABILITY AS HEDGING: None.
SITE AND SOIL: Always best in full sun but will tolerate light shade. The soil must be acidic and free draining; don't grow on alkaline or water-logged soils.
HARDINESS: Very hardy.
SPECIAL CARE: When mulching, use an acidic material such as chopped conifer needles. Regular clipping is worthwhile either immediately after flowering or in early spring as the plants soon become straggly. To propagate, take short semi-ripe cuttings in early summer, or layer.
SIZE: Varies with variety but most are within the range 10-50 x 50-90cm (4in-1¾ft x 1¾-3ft).

SIGNIFICANT PROBLEMS

Roots can rot and stems die back, especially in wet soils. Against widespread opinion, heathers do not grow in bogs.

Calluna vulgaris 'Wickwar Flame'

Recommended Varieties
There are several hundred heather varieties so don't feel restricted by my selection of personal favourites:

'Annemarie' AGM, double deep pink flowers; 'Beoley Gold' AGM, vivid yellow leaves, white flowers; 'County Wicklow' AGM, double pink flowers, compact habit; 'Gold Haze' AGM, golden leaves in summer, gold-bronze in winter, white flowers; 'H. E. Beale' (syn. 'Pink Beale'), double bright rose-pink flowers on tall plants; 'Kinlochruel' AGM, double white flowers, compact habit; 'Peter Sparkes', double rose-pink flowers on long spikes, ideal for cutting and drying; 'Robert Chapman' AGM, golden leaves in spring, changing through orange and bronze to red in winter, purple flowers, an imposing and vigorous tall bush; 'Sir John Charrington' AGM, yellow-gold leaves, turning orange with red shoot tips in winter, dark red flowers, compact and bushy; 'Sunset' AGM, gold-yellow leaves in spring, turning orange in summer, red-bronze in winter, mauve-pink flowers; 'Wickwar Flame' AGM, vivid orange-yellow leaves in summer, vivid red in winter, mauve flowers.

Camellia

" I don't know who conjures up names like 'the Queen of shrubs' but someone did it once for the camellia; and everyone knows what they mean. Ever since Camellia japonica was first introduced into western gardens from China in the early 18th century, these glorious plants have been prized and admired; their rich dark green foliage setting off perfectly the tissue paper flowers. But how many gardeners today appreciate that the wide range of hybrid varieties from which we can now choose are of much more recent origin? Not until C. saluenensis was discovered by George Forrest in 1917 and then used by the great nurseryman J. C. Williams in Cornwall was the potential offered by hybrid camellias first realised. "

FLOWERING or FRUITING INTEREST: Superb flowers in white or shades of red and pink in spring. Many varieties with single, double and semi-double blooms.

FOLIAGE INTEREST: Glossy dark green leaves, some varieties are rather oddly variegated or have 'fishtail' effects.

SUITABILITY AS HEDGING: Only in very mild areas where they could be part of a mixed boundary planting.

SITE AND SOIL: The plants need a lightly shaded position sheltered from cold winds. In cold areas, a more sunny situation is needed to develop the best flowers. The ideal soil is humus-rich and acidic; on alkaline soils growth will be poor and the leaves chlorotic so in these conditions, camellias are best grown in large containers of acidic compost. Flowers can be spoiled if frozen buds warm up quickly in the morning sun, so avoid east-facing positions.

HARDINESS: The plants are fairly to moderately hardy but the early spring buds often damaged by cold winds.

SPECIAL CARE : Once a suitable site has been chosen, the only special care needed is to mulch with garden compost or chopped conifer needles and to give a supplementary feed with sequestered iron in spring. No pruning is necessary but any misplaced shoots should be cut out after flowering. To propagate, take semi-ripe cuttings in autumn or leaf-bud cuttings in spring.

SIZE: Up to 1 x 1m (3 x 3ft) after three years, about 3-4 x 2-3m (10-13 x 6½-10ft) ultimately.

Camellia x williamsii **'Debbie'**

Camellia **'Cornish Snow'**

C. japonica **'Adolphe Audusson'**

SIGNIFICANT PROBLEMS

Aphids, scale insects and sooty moulds can disfigure leaves. Bud drop is usually due to sudden changes in temperature or the soil drying out over the summer or early autumn.

Carpenteria californica AGM

FLOWERING or FRUITING INTEREST: Beautiful white scented flowers with prominent yellow anthers appear in early to midsummer.
FOLIAGE INTEREST: Glossy dark green leaves with white undersides.
SUITABILITY AS HEDGING: None.
SITE AND SOIL: Needs a warm protected site, a sunny sheltered wall is ideal although in mild areas it may be grown in a more open position. Tolerant of most good garden soils.
HARDINESS: Barely to fairly hardy.
SPECIAL CARE: Protect over winter by mulching. No regular pruning is necessary although if the plants becomes too large or flowering is reduced, cut out one third of the stems after flowering. After a hard winter cut back damaged wood. Propagate by softwood cuttings taken in summer.
SIZE: 1 x 1m (3 x 3ft) after about 10 years and rarely attains more than 1.5-3m (5-10ft).

SIGNIFICANT PROBLEMS

Poor flowering and frost damage. Lack of flowers is common in seed-raised plants so try to buy a plant when it is in bloom.

Carpenteria californica

Cassiope

❝ *Cassiope was the wife of Cepheus and the mother of Andromeda in Greek mythology; but just what was the nature of her connection with this small, heather-like shrub is something that no-one has ever been able to tell me. I certainly can't believe that the good lady herself ever saw one for they fall into the category that botanists call 'Arctic-Alpine'; they originate in very cold places. And for that reason, they are among the toughest evergreens that you will grow in your garden. In reality, they make attractive and welcome alternatives to heathers for rather wetter soil; although they do still need the acidity.* ❞

FLOWERING or FRUITING INTEREST: White bell-shaped flowers in spring.
FOLIAGE INTEREST: Dense, overlapping leaves.
SUITABILITY AS HEDGING: None.
SITE AND SOIL: Although these dwarf shrubs are similar in appearance to heathers, they need a more moist acidic soil. They thrive best in cool, open positions and makes good choices for exposed sites.
HARDINESS: Very hardy.
SPECIAL CARE: Remove any brown straggly growths in spring. Take semi-ripe cuttings in late summer or layer.
SIZE: These are slow-growing plants that attain their ultimate size in five years; this varies with species but is unlikely to be more than 30 x 40cm (1 x 1½ft).

SIGNIFICANT PROBLEMS
Plants grown in containers often suffer from vine weevil and red spider mite.

Recommended Varieties
C. 'Edinburgh' AGM, slender dark green stems, one of the biggest and easiest to grow. C. lycopodiodes AGM, prostrate mat 10 x 30cm (4in x 1ft), white flowers; C. l. 'Beatrice Lilley' free-flowering and more compact than the species. C. 'Randle Cook' AGM, mat-like habit, with stems up to 15cm (6in) high.

Cassiope 'Randle Cooke'

Ceanothus
Californian lilac

FLOWERING or FRUITING INTEREST: Clouds of blue flowers usually in late spring/early summer.
FOLIAGE INTEREST: Small leaves, shiny on the upper surface, more dull on the undersides.
SUITABILITY AS HEDGING: None.
SITE AND SOIL: A sheltered sunny or lightly shaded position is needed, and ceanothus are often grown as wall shrubs against a warm wall or fence, but in mild areas can be grown as free-standing specimens. A good garden soil that drains well is ideal; they are unsuccessful on poor sites or thin soils.
HARDINESS: Most types are barely hardy to fairly hardy, but a few are moderately hardy.
SPECIAL CARE: Wall-trained specimens require tying in. Trim back lightly each year after flowering and cut out winter-damaged shoots in spring. Propagate from semi-ripe cuttings in summer.
SIZE: Varies with species and site (wall-trained plants grow larger than free-standing ones). Most attain 2-3m (6½-10ft) but dwarf varieties are available.

SIGNIFICANT PROBLEMS
Hard winters and cold winds can cause damage and they may show signs of chlorosis on thin alkaline soils. This can be corrected by sequestered iron fertiliser.

ABOVE: *Ceanothus prostratus* 'Puget Blue'
RIGHT: *C. arboreus* 'Trewithen Blue'

Recommended Varieties

Size and hardiness vary so choose a plant that is appropriate to the site; the heights I give here are those to be expected after five years only as long-lived plants are rare, even in the very best growing conditions.

C. arboreus 'Trewithen Blue' AGM, barely hardy to fairly hardy, can attain 4m (13ft) or more in mild areas, flowers in spring. *C.* 'Autumnal Blue' AGM, moderately hardy, 1.5m (5ft) flowers in spring and summer/autumn. *C.* 'Blue Mound' AGM, barely hardy to fairly hardy, only 1-1.5m (3-5ft) high but spreads to 1.8m (5¾ft), often flowers in early summer and autumn. *C.* 'Burkwoodii' AGM, barely hardy to fairly hardy, 1.5m (5ft), flowers from late spring to early autumn. *C.* 'Cascade' AGM, barely hardy to fairly hardy, tall at 3m (10ft) or more, pendulous habit with flowers at the tips in late spring makes it ideal for wall training. *C.* 'Concha', 1.8m (5½ft), barely hardy to fairly hardy, flowers red in bud with display in late spring. *C.* 'Cynthia Postan', barely hardy to fairly hardy, 2.4m (6¾ft), flowers in late spring/early summer.

C. impressus, barely hardy to fairly hardy, 1.5 x 1.5-2.4m (5 x 5-6¾ft), flowers in late spring. *C.* 'Italian Skies' AGM, barely hardy to fairly hardy, among the taller varieties at 3m (10ft), flowers in late spring. *C. prostratus* 'Puget Blue' AGM, barely hardy to fairly hardy, 2-3m (6½-10 ft) tall, flowers in early summer. *C.* 'Southmead' AGM, barely hardy to fairly hardy, 1.5m (5ft), flowers late spring/early summer. *C. thyrsiflorus repens* (syn. *C. repens*), AGM, moderately hardy, good ground cover as only about 75cm (2½ft) high, flowers in mid/late spring.

Choisya ternata AGM Mexican orange blossom

❝ One of the great and frustrating mysteries of gardening over the past decade or so has been why we have developed an obsession with so-called 'golden' variants of otherwise perfectly sound green-leaved plants. There's no better example of this than Choisya*; if there is to be one message from this book, it must be to bring back the genuinely original form of this charming species. ❞*

FLOWERING or FRUITING INTEREST: Small, orange-scented, star-like flowers in early summer; less on the variety 'Sundance'.

FOLIAGE INTEREST: Glossy, dark green leaves pleasantly scented if crushed. A yellow-leaved variety also available.

SUITABILITY AS HEDGING: None.

SITE AND SOIL Tolerates both full sun or moderate shade, best when sheltered from cold winds. Any fairly good garden soil is suitable.

HARDINESS: Moderately hardy.

SPECIAL CARE: Cut back the oldest one-third of the shoots to soil level each year after flowering. To propagate, take semi-ripe cuttings in late summer.

SIZE: 1 x 1m (3 x 3ft) in the early years, about double this ultimately.

Choisya 'Aztec Pearl'

SIGNIFICANT PROBLEMS

None although *C. t.* 'Sundance' can scorch in hot sun or turn green in dense shade.

Recommended Varieties
The normal species is the one most usually grown as a garden plant. There are also two increasingly widely grown variants with additional features. *C.* 'Aztec Pearl' AGM, attractively shaped leaves as each leaf is more divided than those of the species and the flower buds have a pretty pink tinge to them but the flowers are not as strongly fragrant. *C. t.* 'Sundance' AGM, bright yellow leaves and fewer flowers, a plant that has become very popular for reasons that elude me.

Cistus Rock rose, Sun rose

FLOWERING or FRUITING INTEREST: Saucer-shaped flowers, usually white or pink, in early to midsummer. Although each bloom is short-lived the flowers are produced in abundance.

FOLIAGE INTEREST: Grey-green or dark green leaves.

SUITABILITY AS HEDGING: None.

SITE AND SOIL: These are plants of the Mediterranean so need full sun, shelter from cold winds, and a light, free-draining soil. They thrive in alkaline soils in mild coastal gardens, or on sunny sandy banks or rock gardens.

HARDINESS: Barely hardy to moderately hardy.

SPECIAL CARE: Dead-head to encourage flowering. Protect over winter. Pruning should be restricted to trimming away winter damage in spring but avoid cutting into old wood. To propagate, take semi-ripe cuttings in summer or hardwood cuttings in winter. Some species can be raised successfully from seed.

SIZE: These tend to be short-lived

Cistus 'Peggy Sammons'

shrubs growing to about 1 x 1m (3 x 3ft) after five years although the size does varies with species.

SIGNIFICANT PROBLEMS

None if they are sited correctly to avoid shade, wet clay soils and cold winds.

Recommended Varieties

C. x aguilarii 'Maculatus', fairly hardy, large flowers with a central ring of crimson around a yellow centre. *C. x cyprius* (syn. *C. ladanifer*) AGM, moderately hardy, grows to 2 m (6½ft), white flowers with crimson blotches, grey-green leaves. *C. x dansereaui* 'Decumbens' AGM, fairly hardy, spreading habit, 60cm x 1.2m (2 x 4ft), large white flowers with crimson blotch, dark green leaves. *C. x hybridus* (syns. *C. x corbariensis*, *C. coeris*) AGM, fairly hardy, white flowers with yellow blotches, red in bud, dark green leaves. *C. ladanifer* AGM, fairly hardy, tall up to 2.4m (6¾ft), large white flowers with chocolate brown-purple stain around yellow stamens, crumpled petals, dark green leaves. *C.* 'Peggy Sammons' AGM, moderately hardy, delicate pink flowers, grey-green leaves. *C. x purpureus* AGM, fairly hardy, the flowers are impressive, large rose-pink flowers with maroon blotches and yellow stamens, dark grey-green leaves, red stems. *C.* 'Silver Pink', moderately hardy, long inflorescences of silver-pink flowers, pale green leaves with grey undersides. *C. x skanbergii* AGM, fairly hardy, clear pink flowers, grey-green leaves.

Convolvulus cneorum

FLOWERING or FRUITING INTEREST: White or pale pink flowers similar to those of bindweed appear in early summer.

FOLIAGE INTEREST: Silver leaves that look their most spectacular in spring and summer when very few plants have leaves of a more intense silver.

SUITABILITY AS HEDGING: None.

SITE AND SOIL: Full sun with shelter from cold winds and a light, well-drained soil are essential; cold wet soils are fatal. Ideal for sunny flower beds and rock gardens.

Convolvulus cneorum

HARDINESS: Fairly hardy to moderately hardy.

SPECIAL CARE: Very lightly prune out misplaced shoots in spring. Take care not to leave branch stubs as these seem to be infected very readily by decay fungi. To propagate, take semi-ripe cuttings in early summer or sow seed.

SIZE: 45 x 45 cm (1½ x 1½ft) after three to five years, ultimately 75 x 75cm (2½ x 2½ft).

SIGNIFICANT PROBLEMS

None.

Recommended Varieties

Only the true species is available.

Corokia

" Corokia *is a New Zealand plant; Corokia indeed is a Maori name. And as such it joins a select group of representatives of that country's quite magnificent flora that thrive well in European gardens. It is a great frustration to northern gardeners that relatively few can tolerate the worst of our winters and even these species really need a sheltered position. But given a degree of shelter, they are immensely rewarding; and the genus includes in the confusingly named* C. cotoneaster, *a plant that comes closer to metalwork than anything else in botany.* "

FLOWERING or FRUITING INTEREST: Small, star-like yellow flowers from late spring to early summer. In autumn, small spherical fruits appear in various colours depending on the species.

FOLIAGE INTEREST: Varies with species.

SUITABILITY AS HEDGING: None except named varieties of *C.* x *virgata* in mild areas.

SITE AND SOIL: A well drained soil and a sheltered sunny site are required. These plants are best suited to mild areas or to being grown in containers and then brought under cover for winter.

HARDINESS: Barely hardy to fairly hardy.

SPECIAL CARE: These are slow-growing plants and pruning is rarely necessary. To propagate take semi-ripe cuttings in autumn.

SIZE: Some can attain 2 x 1-1.5m (6½ x 3-5ft) after five to 10 years.

SIGNIFICANT PROBLEMS
None.

Corokia buddlejoides

Recommended Varieties
C. buddlejoides, erect habit, shiny leaves with white undersides, dark red fruits that remain over winter. *C. cotoneaster*, one of the hardiest and smallest at 60-90cm (2-3ft), stiff wiry branches that interconnect giving the remarkable appearance of wire-netting, small leaves, orange-red fruits. *C.* x *virgata*, a variable hybrid, leaves can be bronze, green or grey and fruits yellow, orange or red.

Coronilla valentina glauca AGM

FLOWERING or FRUITING INTEREST: Scented, yellow, pea-like flowers are at their peak from late spring to early summer but flowering continues intermittently until the autumn frosts.

FOLIAGE INTEREST: Blue-grey leaves composed of rounded leaflets.

SUITABILITY AS HEDGING: None.

SITE AND SOIL: Requires a sunny, sheltered site and is often fan-trained against a fence. Tolerates almost all garden soils, even if fairly strongly alkaline.

HARDINESS: Barely hardy to fairly hardy.

SPECIAL CARE: To encourage new shoots to grow for tying in, cut back a few of the oldest branches to soil level each year. To propagate, take softwood or semi-ripe cuttings in summer or sow seed.

SIZE: 1.5 x 1.5m (5 x 5ft) after five years, 2 x 2m (6½ x 6½ft) after 10 years.

SIGNIFICANT PROBLEMS
None.

Coronilla valentina glauca 'Citrina'

Recommended Varieties
C. v. g. 'Citrina' AGM, pale lemon flowers; *C. v. g.* 'Variegata', cream-white edges to the leaves, more tender than the parent.

Crinodendron hookerianum (syn. *Tricuspidaria lanceolata*) AGM Lantern tree

FLOWERING or FRUITING INTEREST: Buds appear in autumn and remain over winter until the dark red lantern-like flowers appear in late spring and early summer.

FOLIAGE INTEREST: Narrow leathery leaves.

SUITABILITY AS HEDGING: None.

SITE AND SOIL: A warm sheltered position in light shade with an acidic moist soil. Alternatively, grow it in a container as a conservatory plant but take care to keep the roots cool and moist.

HARDINESS: Barely hardy to fairly hardy.

SPECIAL CARE: No routine pruning is necessary but to keep the plant vigorous and neat, cut out the oldest one-third of the shoots after flowering. To propagate take softwood cuttings in early summer.

SIZE: Can be slow to establish but then attains 3 x 2m (10 x 6½ft) after 10 years and ultimately much more.

SIGNIFICANT PROBLEMS
Leaves scorch in full sun or cold winds.

Recommended Varieties
C. hookerianum is the hardiest species but a related plant is *C. patagua* (syn. *Tricuspidaria dependens*) which is similar in size but has white bell-shaped flowers in late summer. It is barely hardy and can only be grown outdoors in mild areas.

Crinodendron patagua

Cotoneaster

❝ *On page 26, I described a shrub called* Corokia cotoneaster; *here we have the real thing, a genus of around 50 species and one that is of immense horticultural merit, both in its deciduous and its evergreen types.* Cotoneaster *is a member of the rose family and, like roses themselves, botanically very confusing for many species are able to set seed without being fertilised with the result that seedlings can vary greatly even when originating from the same parent. Despite the great merits of the genus, I still believe that most gardeners never see more than a handful of* Cotoneaster *species, as much as anything because the majority of garden centres only stock the most popular. So although the herringbone plant,* C. horizontalis *may be a wonderful thing in its way, do please explore the evergreens too.* ❞

FLOWERING or FRUITING
INTEREST: White blossom in spring or early summer; rather uniform across a large number of otherwise different species. Red or yellow spherical fruits in autumn.

FOLIAGE INTEREST: Dark green to grey-green leaves, some late season colour from the red older leaves.

SUITABILITY AS HEDGING: Most of the medium and tall forms can be used as informal hedges.

SITE AND SOIL: Full sun to moderate shade. Any fairly good garden soil is suitable but they are least successful on shallow, dry alkaline sites. Most are ideal plants for windy exposed gardens. The wide range of sizes and habits mean there is a type for most garden sites including rock gardens, wall plantings against cool, shady walls or fences, as standards or ground cover.

HARDINESS: Very hardy.

SPECIAL CARE: No pruning is necessary although plants that become too large for their allotted positions should be pruned lightly in spring. To propagate take semi-ripe cuttings in summer or hardwood cuttings in winter. Low-growing types can be layered.

SIZE: Low-growing types remain at 50cm (1¾ft) but spread from 1m (3ft) after five years to 3m (10ft) ultimately. Medium types attain 1 x 1.5m (3 x 5ft) after five years and 1.5 x 4m (5 x 13ft) ultimately. Taller types attain 3 x 2.5m (10 x 8ft) after five years and twice this ultimately. Many can very successfully be trained as standards.

SIGNIFICANT PROBLEMS
Fireblight.

Cotoneaster congestus

Cotoneaster dammeri

Cotoneaster salicifolius **'Exburyensis'**

Recommended Varieties

C. cochleatus AGM, low growing, glossy dark green leaves.
C. congestus, low-growing, dense, creeping habit, dark blue-green leaves, early summer flowers, red fruits. *C. c.* 'Nana', ideal for rock gardens as only attains 5 x 50cm (2in x 1¾ft). *C. conspicuus* 'Decorus' AGM, low to medium height, arching habit, grey-green leaves, spring flowers, red fruits. *C. dammeri* AGM, low growing, ideal ground cover as the stems root into the soil, dark green to red leaves, summer flowers, dark red fruits. *C. franchetii*, medium height with arching habit, dark grey-green leaves, summer flowers, dark red fruits. *C. lacteus* AGM, tall, dark green leaves, summer flowers, dark red fruits. *C. microphyllus* AGM, low-growing mound, tiny dark green leaves, summer flowers, large red fruits. *C. salicifolius* 'Exburyensis', tall, mid-green leaves, summer flowers, pale yellow fruits; *C. s.* 'Pendulus' (syn. 'Hybridus Pendulus'), often grown as a grafted weeping standard or as ground cover; *C. s.* 'Rothschildianus' AGM semi-evergreen with light green willow-like leaves, cream yellow fruits. *C.* x *suecicus* 'Coral Beauty', low growing but spreading habit used as ground cover or wall shrub, coral red fruits.

29

Cyathodes colensoi

> ❝ *The plant family Epacridaceae is another of the splendours from the southern hemisphere that finds its way into European gardening through a minute sample of its compass. It is related to the Ericaceae and, like that family, many of its members require acidic soils. But many are too tender for us and* Cyathodes colensoi *is almost the only species that we can grow.* ❞

FLOWERING or FRUITING INTEREST: Small white tubular flowers carried on tips in spring. Both male and female plants need to be grown close together to give a chance of obtaining the white, pink or red fruits.

FOLIAGE INTEREST: The new growth is pink and contrasts strikingly with the blue-green older leaves.

SUITABILITY AS HEDGING: None

SITE AND SOIL: Requires an acidic soil with abundant humus to produce conditions that are moist but well drained. The plant needs a sheltered position in partial shade although it can tolerate more sun when grown in cooler conditions.

HARDINESS: Fairly hardy to barely hardy

SPECIAL CARE: Cut off straggly shoots after flowering. To propagate, take semi-ripe cuttings in summer.

SIZE: 20 x 30cm (8in x 1ft) after five years, ultimately 45cm (1½ft) high.

SIGNIFICANT PROBLEMS
None.

Cyathodes colensoi

Recommended Varieties
Only this species can be grown in Britain.

Daboecia cantabrica   Irish heath, St Dabeoc's heath

FLOWERING or FRUITING INTEREST: Small hanging purple-pink flowers in early summer and again in autumn.

FOLIAGE INTEREST: Glossy dark green leaves with white undersides.

SUITABILITY AS HEDGING: None.

SITE AND SOIL: An acidic or neutral soil with abundant humus to produce moist but well-drained conditions. It will thrive in an open site in sun or light shade but avoid frost pockets. Effective when grown as ground cover between dwarf conifers or acid-loving shrubs.

HARDINESS: Very hardy but can suffer some damage in frost pockets and wet soils.

SPECIAL CARE: Don't allow to dry out in the first season. Prune back to the base of the dead flowers in spring. It is easy to propagate from shoot-tip cuttings in summer or if layered like a heather.

SIZE: 40 x 70cm (1½ x 2¼ft).

SIGNIFICANT PROBLEMS
None.

Recommended Varieties
The species is widely grown but the following varieties offer variations in flower colour:
D. c. alba, white; *D. c.* 'Bicolor' AGM, white, pink and purple flowers on the same plant; *D. c.* 'Praegerae', deep cerise-purple; will shed its leaves in cold winters.

Daboecia cantabrica

Danae racemosa (syn. *Ruscus racemosus*) AGM Alexandrian laurel

FLOWERING or FRUITING INTEREST: Not a great deal: bright red fruits form in autumn following hot summers. Male and female flowers are on the same plant. The only other plant that you are likely to see that is remotely similar is *Ruscus aculeatus* (page 66). Flower arrangers love them both.

FOLIAGE INTEREST: Glossy green flattened stems on arching shoots take the place of true leaves.

SUITABILITY AS HEDGING: Can make a rather good low hedge used in much the same way as box.

SITE AND SOIL: Most suitable for sites such as deep shade and dry soil where few plants will thrive although will be better in more moist, richer soil and some sun.

HARDINESS: Fairly hardy to moderately hardy.

SPECIAL CARE: Slow-growing initially. No pruning necessary but the oldest one-third of the shoots may be cut from mature plants in spring to rejuvenate them. Unusually for a shrub, *Danae* may be divided in the same way as a herbaceous perennial.

SIZE: 50cm x 1m (1¾ x 3ft) after five years, double this ultimately.

SIGNIFICANT PROBLEMS
None.

Recommended Varieties
This true species is the only form available.

Danae racemosa

31

Daphne

Some of the greatest pleasures of my student days were the regular field trips to study our native plant life. Sometimes the plants we found and examined were relatively commonplace; sometimes, usually because we were visiting an uncommon or unfamiliar type of habitat, they were more unusual and striking. And sometimes a finding was in a rather special category that stayed in the memory. My first encounter with our two native species of Daphne *in an area of old and undisturbed limestone woodland was just such an occasion. We found the deciduous* D. mezereum *and the evergreen* D. laureola *growing within a few metres of each other. Both species have been in all of my gardens since, where they have been joined by some of the quietly lovely Asiatic species.*

Daphne blagayana

FLOWERING or FRUITING INTEREST: Clusters of sweet-scented pink or white flowers from winter to late spring. Some have poisonous fruits in late summer.

FOLIAGE INTEREST: Grey-green or glossy green leaves in attractive rosettes. Some types are variegated.

SUITABILITY AS HEDGING: None.

SITE AND SOIL: Varies with species; some require sun, some are very valuable shade plants. All require a deep loamy soil enriched with humus to provide moist but well drained conditions. Daphnes establish slowly and are then best not moved.

HARDINESS: Most are fairly hardy to moderately hardy.

SPECIAL CARE: Use compost or, even better, conifer needles as a mulch. No pruning is necessary, remove any misshapen growths in early spring. Tricky to propagate, take semi-ripe cuttings in summer or alternatively layer low-growing types.

SIZE: Varies with species but most are 50 x 50cm (1¾ x 1¾ft) after five years, ultimately double this.

SIGNIFICANT PROBLEMS

May be weak growing, but this is thought to be due to virus so avoid plants with mottles or flecks on the leaves and control aphid attacks promptly. In time, they suffer dieback so are not long lived.

Recommended Varieties

D. blagayana, only 10-30cm (4in-1ft) tall, mat-like habit, sweet scented cream-white flowers in spring, grey-green leaves, best in partial shade. *D. x burkwoodii* AGM, semi-evergreen, one of the bigger types at 1-1.5m (3-5ft) in height, rounded habit, scented purple-pink and white flowers from late spring to early summer. *D. cneorum*, low spreading habit to 20 x 75cm (8in x 2½ft), scented rose-pink flowers from late spring to early summer, green leaves with grey undersides. *D. laureola*, upright habit, the glossy green leaves are the main feature as the honey-scented flowers are small and yellow-green, black fruits, ideal for dry shade. *D. odora*, makes a bush 1.2m (4ft) or more, barely hardy to bairly hardy, dark green leaves, scented red-purple flowers; *D. o.* 'Aureomarginata' (syns. 'Marginata', *D. japonica* 'Striata'), leaves have a narrow yellow margin which ages to cream-white, hardier than the all-green species, an unusual feature to find in a variegated plant. *D. pontica* AGM, 1 x 1m (3 x 3ft), honey-scented yellow-green flowers in spring, glossy green leaves, thrives well in shade. *D. tangutica* AGM, scented pale pink-purple, white tinged flowers in late spring to early summer, deep green leathery leaves.

Desfontainia spinosa AGM

**FLOWERING or FRUITING
INTEREST:** Strikingly distinctive long
tubular flowers that are red with yellow
tips. Mid- to late summer.
FOLIAGE INTEREST: Glossy, spiny
leaves of dark green; very reminiscent of
holly.
SUITABILITY AS HEDGING: None.
SITE AND SOIL: Best in a sheltered
site in partial shade. A deep acidic soil
with abundant humus is ideal and the
plant is intolerant of heavy, alkaline or
water-logged soils.
HARDINESS Fairly hardy.
SPECIAL CARE: When mulching, use

Desfontainia spinosa

an acidic material such as conifer needles.
No routine pruning is necessary. The
easiest way to propagate is by removing
suckers but semi-ripe cuttings can also
be taken in early summer and it may be
successfully raised from ripe seed.
SIZE: 75 x 50cm (2½ x 1¾ft) after five
years, ultimately it can attain 2.4 x 1.5m
(6¾ x 5ft)

SIGNIFICANT PROBLEMS
None.

> **Recommended Varieties**
> The true species is as good as the
> few named varieties sometimes
> offered.

Drimys winteri Winter's bark

**FLOWERING or FRUITING
INTEREST:** Scented white flowers in
spring but only on fairly mature plants.
FOLIAGE INTEREST: The leaves and
bark are aromatic.
SUITABILITY AS HEDGING: None.
SITE AND SOIL: Partial shade in an
acidic soil enriched with humus so it is
well-drained yet moist.
HARDINESS: Fairly hardy to moderately hardy.
SPECIAL CARE: When mulching use
an acidic material such as conifer needles.
SIZE: 2 x 2m (6½ x 6½ft) after five years,
ultimately 10 x 4m (30 x 13ft).

SIGNIFICANT PROBLEMS
None.

> **Recommended Varieties**
> The true species is the best.

Drimys winteri

Erica carnea Heather and Heaths

❝ *Mainly I suppose because their leaves are so small, ericas aren't usually thought of as evergreen shrubs. It is their flowers that attract attention; the foliage is, quite literally, overlooked. And individually, an* Erica *leaf will certainly never win prizes but collectively they do form a neat carpet against which the flowers are more strikingly displayed. Gardeners who enjoy heathers but who garden on alkaline soil should look here, rather than in the true heather genus* Calluna *for they will find among the winter-flowering (in reality autumn to spring flowering) species and varieties a great many that will tolerate their soil conditions.* ❞

Erica carnea 'Foxhollow'

Recommended Varieties
There is an ever-changing range of varieties available from garden centres and nurseries but do take account both of flower and leaf colours when making your selection. The following varieties are among those that I have found especially reliable.

E. carnea (syn. *E. herbacea*) varieties are winter-flowering heathers that tolerate alkalinity: 'Ann Sparkes' AGM, orange-and-yellow leaves with red tips in spring, deep red flowers, only spreads to 25cm (10in); 'Foxhollow' AGM, vivid golden-yellow leaves that become more intense in winter and develop red tints, sparse pale pink flowers; 'King George', bright rose-pink flowers; 'Myretoun Ruby' AGM, crimson flowers, one of the best reds; 'Pink Spangles' AGM, shell-pink flowers that deepen as they age, trailing habit; 'Springwood White' AGM, bright green leaves, white flowers, trailing habit to 60cm (2ft); 'Vivellii' AGM, deep green-bronze leaves, dark red flowers.

E. cinerea varieties are summer and autumn-flowering heathers that require an acidic soil: 'Alba Minor' AGM, bright green leaves, white flowers, compact; 'Eden Valley' AGM, mid-green leaves, lavender and white flowers; 'Pink Ice' AGM, only 15cm (6in) tall but spreads to 35cm (1¼ft), clear rose-pink flowers.

FLOWERING or FRUITING INTEREST: Masses of small, bell-like flowers (although larger than those of *Calluna*), usually pinks, purple, red or white.

FOLIAGE INTEREST: Narrow, needle-like leaves in colourful shades of green or yellow, many have very beautiful winter tints.

SUITABILITY AS HEDGING: None except perhaps the tall *E. erigena* types.

SITE AND SOIL: Full sun to partial shade. The soil should be free-draining and, for most types, acidic although *E. carnea* and *E. x darleyensis* especially are alkalinity tolerant. Ideal plants for exposed sites.

HARDINESS: The species recommended here are all hardy.

SPECIAL CARE: Mulch with an acidic material such as conifer needles. Regular annual trimming after flowering prevents the plants from becoming leggy. If you use one-handed shears to do this, you can hold the tuft of shoots with your free hand. To propagate, take semi-ripe cuttings in early summer.

SIZE: Most attain their full size of 30-50 x 50-75cm (1-1¾ x1¾-2½ft) within three years.

SIGNIFICANT PROBLEMS
None.

Erica cinerea 'Alba Minor'

Erica vagans 'Mrs D. F. Maxwell'

E. x darleyensis varieties flower between winter and spring and are moderately lime-tolerant: 'Arthur Johnson' AGM, green leaves with cream tips in spring, long spikes of pink flowers, slightly scented; 'Furzey' AGM, green leaves with pink tips in spring, mauve-pink flowers; 'Ghost Hills' AGM, light green leaves with cream tips in spring, pink flowers; 'Jack H. Brummage', yellow leaves in summer, orange-bronze in winter, mauve-pink flowers.

Others
E. erigena (syns. *E. hibernica*, *E. mediterranea*), spring flowers highly attractive to bees, fairly alkalinity tolerant: 'Golden Lady' AGM, carpeting habit, bright yellow leaves, sparse white flowers, scorched by cold winds, 30 x 40cm (1 x ½ft); 'W. T. Rackcliff' AGM, bright green leaves, white flowers, 75 x 60cm (2½ x 2ft).

E. tetralix 'Con Underwood', needs an acidic moist soil, hummock-forming, grey-green leaves, red flowers in summer/autumn.

E. vagans varieties have summer to autumn flowers. Despite what is sometimes said, in my experience requires acidic soil: 'Lyonesse' AGM, bright green leaves, white flowers; 'Mrs D. F. Maxwell' AGM, dark green leaves, light rose-pink flowers.

Elaeagnus

" *Among the endless pleasures of gardening is the fact that it can always spring surprises. And no surprise was more pleasant than when, after several years of growing a number of evergreen species of* Elaeagnus, *one that I had thought of simply as a good ground-smothering foliage plant, produced a crop of beautiful little fruits. I vowed never to think of the genus as commonplace or workaday again.* "

FLOWERING or FRUITING INTEREST: Inconspicuous but sweetly-scented yellow flowers in late summer, followed by very beautiful small orange fruits, especially in hot seasons.

FOLIAGE INTEREST: Most have gold variegation that becomes especially pronounced in winter.

SUITABILITY AS HEDGING: A good informal windbreak.

SITE AND SOIL: Full sun to moderate shade, thrives well on most garden soils except those that are very alkaline; moderate alkalinity is tolerated. Very good for coastal gardens.

HARDINESS: Hardy.

SPECIAL CARE: No pruning necessary but one-third of the older shoots may be cut to soil level in spring. If variegated plants produce any all-green shoots, these should be cut out promptly. Those grown as hedges should be lightly trimmed in late spring.

SIZE: 1 x 1m (3 x 3ft) after five years, can attain 4 x 3m (13 x 10ft) ultimately.

SIGNIFICANT PROBLEMS
None.

Elaeagnus x *ebbingei* 'Gilt Edge'

Recommended Varieties
E. x *ebbingei*, oval grey-green leaves; 'Coastal Gold', golden yellow leaves with green margins and silver undersides, fragrant small white flowers in autumn followed by orange fruits; 'Gilt Edge', AGM, broad gold edges to leaves. *E. pungens* green shiny leaves with dull white undersides; 'Frederici', very narrow, pointed light green leaves with cream-white blotches, slow growing; 'Maculata' (syn. 'Aureovariegata') AGM, dark green leaves with irregular gold blotches, very easy and very reliable; 'Variegata' (syn. 'Argenteovariegata') AGM, mid-green leaves with white-yellow edges.

Eriobotrya japonica AGM Loquat, Japanese medlar

FLOWERING or FRUITING INTEREST: Little of interest when grown in Britain but in its native habitat, inflorescences of scented hawthorn-like flowers are intermittently produced from winter to spring followed by edible yellow fruit.

FOLIAGE INTEREST: Leathery corrugated leaves often 30cm (1ft) long. The leaves are dark green and the undersides are covered in brown hairs; the leaf is really quite unlike anything else in British gardens.

SUITABILITY AS HEDGING: None.

SITE AND SOIL: A sunny sheltered position; it is often grown against a suitable sunny wall. The soil should be fertile and well drained.

HARDINESS: Barely hardy to fairly hardy.

SPECIAL CARE: No pruning is necessary but misshapen branches should be removed in winter. Propagate by seeds sown in spring or summer.

SIZE: 1.5 x 1m (5 x 3ft) after five years, ultimately 8m (25ft).

SIGNIFICANT PROBLEMS
None.

Recommended Varieties
The normal species is the form most likely to be seen.

Eriobotrya japonica

Escallonia

FLOWERING or FRUITING INTEREST: Clusters of pink or red flowers are at their peak in early summer but continue on and off until the autumn.

FOLIAGE INTEREST: Dark green glossy leaves.

SUITABILITY AS HEDGING: A very useful windbreak in mild and coastal areas.

SITE AND SOIL: Tolerates sun or light shade in any well-drained garden soil. Some types need shelter from cold winds and frost so are best grown close to a warm wall or fence.

HARDINESS: Varies with type, most are fairly hardy to moderately hardy.

SPECIAL CARE: No pruning necessary but straggly growth should be cut out after flowering. Those such as *E. rubra*

Recommended Varieties
E. 'Apple blossom' AGM, pink and white flowers, very useful for hedging, only 1 x 1m (3 x 3ft) after five years. E. 'Donard Seedling', white flowers with pink tinge. E. 'Edinensis' AGM, deep pink buds open to pale pink flowers, compact habit. E. 'Iveyi' AGM, white flowers in branched inflorescences appear in mid-late summer, not as hardy as most so requires a warm wall. E. 'Peach Blossom' AGM, pale pink flowers. E. rubra 'Crimson Spire' AGM, bright crimson flowers, a good hedging plant; E. r. var. macrantha, bright red flowers, leaves aromatic when crushed, a vigorous form, ultimately attaining 4m (13ft) and a good hedging plant.

var. *macrantha* grown as hedging plants should be trimmed after flowering or cut back hard in early summer. To propagate take semi-ripe cuttings in summer.

SIZE: Most are within the range 1.2-1.5 ultimately attaining 2-3m (6½-10 ft).

SIGNIFICANT PROBLEMS
Top growth will be damaged by hard frosts or cold winter wind but the plants should re-grow from the base by early summer. For this reason it's unwise to use it as a hedge in colder regions.

Euonymus

❝Euonymus *and* Elaeagnus *(page 36) have much in common. Both are familiar, both may produce fruits when you least expect it, and both have invaluable roles to play in the garden. But it is a species of* Euonymus *that still gives rise to much amusement when I tell people that for more years than I care to remember, I have known it by the name accorded it by one my tutors. To me,* Euonymus japonicus *will always be the public lavatory bush; simply because for reasons that aren't entirely obvious, it is planted more than any other screening plant around public lavatories. None of which of course should stop you from having it and its relatives in your garden.* ❞

**FLOWERING or FRUITING
INTEREST:** Inconspicuous flowers in early summer followed by pink fruits although these are usually only produced in Britain after hot summers when they can be very striking.
FOLIAGE INTEREST: Leaves have very good white or gold leaf variegations.
SUITABILITY AS HEDGING:
E. japonicus is a useful screen in coastal areas.
SITE AND SOIL: Full sun to partial or moderate shade, tolerates most garden soils including alkaline sites.
HARDINESS: Moderately hardy although *E. japonicus* types need protection from late spring frosts.
SPECIAL CARE: Remove misplaced shoots and congested branches in the spring. Those grown as hedges are best

clipped twice a year in midsummer and early autumn. To propagate, take softwood cuttings in early summer.
SIZE: Varies with variety: *E. fortunei* will attain its maximum height of 50cm (1¾ft) after three years than spread slowly to 3m (10ft); *E. japonicus* will attain 1 x 1m

(3 x 3ft) after three years and 4 x 3m (13 x 10ft) ultimately.

SIGNIFICANT PROBLEMS
Powdery mildew on *E. japonicus*.

***Euonymus fortunei* 'Emerald Gaiety'**

Euonymus japonicus **'Microphyllus Albovariegatus'**

Fabiana imbricata

FLOWERING or FRUITING INTEREST: Plumes of white or lavender coloured tubular flowers in early summer. Light green pods in autumn.

FOLIAGE INTEREST: Tiny mid-green leaves give the plant a heather or heath-like appearance.

SUITABILITY AS HEDGING: None; not sufficiently hardy to be trusted.

SITE AND SOIL: Warm, sheltered position such as a sunny wall in mild areas. It thrives best in a moist but well-drained soil but will tolerate most garden soils other than shallow, alkaline conditions.

HARDINESS: Barely hardy.

SPECIAL CARE: No pruning necessary. To propagate, take semi-ripe cuttings in summer.

SIZE: 80 x 60cm (2½ x 2ft) after five years, ultimately 2.4 x 2.4 m (6¾ x 6¾ft).

SIGNIFICANT PROBLEMS
None.

Fabiana imbricata

x *Fatshedera lizei* AGM

" Some plants simply seem made for certain types of garden and would be wholly inappropriate anywhere else. This is one of them. It has an exotic, tropical appearance that belies its suitability for outdoor locations. And this is why a garden with the 'outdoor room' feel so beloved of garden designers is where it will be most appreciated. A small courtyard garden suits it wonderfully whereas in a woodland setting it would be like a fish out of water. "

FLOWERING or FRUITING INTEREST: Inconspicuous green flowers are present more or less all year.
FOLIAGE INTEREST: Very large, glossy, bright green leaves which can attain 15cm (6in) in diameter and are very striking. This is a deceptive shrub, looking like a house plant which it often is, and tender, which it certainly isn't.
SUITABILITY AS HEDGING: None.
SITE AND SOIL: Light to deep shade in a sheltered position. Any garden soil will suffice but it invariably thrives best in a deep fairly rich loam.
HARDINESS: Fairly hardy to moderately hardy.
SPECIAL CARE: Train as wall shrub or against supports, pinching out the growing tips to encourage a bushy habit. Pruning is not necessary except to remove any misshapen branches in spring. To propagate, take softwood cuttings in early summer.
SIZE: 1 x 1.5m (3 x 5ft) after three years about 1.5 x 5m (5 x 16ft) ultimately.

SIGNIFICANT PROBLEMS
None.

x Fatshedera lizei

Recommended Varieties
The normal green-leaved hybrid is the form usually seen although there are some slightly more tender variegated forms, most notably 'Variegata' AGM which has green leaves with white edges and yellow veins.

Fatsia japonica Castor oil plant

FLOWERING or FRUITING INTEREST: Masses of green-white flowers for much of the year, followed by bunches of black fruits from autumn onwards.
FOLIAGE INTEREST: Large leaves up to 50cm (1¾ft) long, glossy bright green and many-lobed.
SUITABILITY AS HEDGING: None.
SITE AND SOIL: Light to deep shade in most garden soils but best in a deep fertile loam.
HARDINESS: Fairly hardy to moderately hardy, the variegated types barely hardy.
SPECIAL CARE: No pruning necessary but may, if necessary, be cut back hard in spring. To propagate take softwood cuttings in early summer.
SIZE: 1 x 1m (3 x 3ft) after three years, ultimately 4 x 4m (13 x 13ft).

SIGNIFICANT PROBLEMS
None.

Recommended Varieties
The normal green-leaved variety of *F. japonica* is best for the garden; there is a variegated form 'Variegata' with cream-white areas on the leaves but it is only really worth growing outdoors in mild areas.

Fatsia japonica 'Variegata'

Gaultheria

**FLOWERING or FRUITING
INTEREST:** Bell-shaped white flowers
from late spring to early summer. Showy
pink, red, blue, purple or white fruits
appear in autumn and last through winter.
FOLIAGE INTEREST: Small leathery
dark green leaves.
SUITABILITY AS HEDGING: Little,
although can be included in a mixed ornamental hedge where effectiveness of a
barrier isn't important.
SITE AND SOIL: Sun or partial shade
in acidic soil which should be moist in
summer but well drained in winter.
HARDINESS: Fairly hardy to moderately hardy.
SPECIAL CARE: G. mucronata is best
planted in groups of three including a
male to ensure the best fruit production.
Trace suckers back to their point of origin and pull them out.
SIZE: Varies with species.

SIGNIFICANT PROBLEMS
None.

Gaultheria x *wisleyensis* 'Wisley
Pearl'

Recommended Varieties
G. cuneata AGM, white flowers from
late summer to early autumn, white
fruits, good ground cover, 20-30cm
x 2m (8in-1ft x 6½ft). *G. mucronata*
(syn. *Pernettya mucronata*) AGM,
white flowers from late spring to
early summer, fruits on female plants
in various colours, suckering ground
cover, 60cm-1.5m x 1.5m (2-5 x 5ft);
'Bell's Seedling' AGM, self-fertile with
deep red fruits, red young stems;
'Crimsonia' AGM, large carmine-red
fruits; 'Pink Pearl', lilac-pink fruits. *G.
procumbens* AGM, creeping species,
glossy dark green leaves, pink-white
flowers in mid- to late summer followed by dark red fruits, 15 x 90cm
(6in-3ft). *G. shallon*, tolerates deep
shade, white flowers tinged with pink
in late spring to early summer, red to
dark purple fruits in autumn, an
aggressive thicket-forming shrub,
like several other species, often used
as game cover, hence the common
name of partridge berry sometimes
applied to gaultherias, useful therefore in wilder gardens but a nuisance
in small ones. 1 x 1.5m (3 x 5ft).
G. x wisleyensis (syn. x *Gaulnettya
wisleyensis*) 'Wisley Pearl', white
flowers in late spring early summer,
deep red fruits, 1 x 1.5m (3 x 5ft).

Griselinia littoralis AGM

" *Littoralis means 'of the sea-shore' and that is where this plant grows naturally in its original home of New Zealand. And undoubtedly, that is where it grows best in Britain too, although whether plants such as this are simply tolerant of the salt-laden air or really thrive on it is arguable.* Griselinia *can be grown in inland areas but the climate must be very mild or those quite beautiful soft green leaves will be browned.* "

FLOWERING or FRUITING INTEREST: None.

FOLIAGE INTEREST: Oval, slightly wavy bright green leaves; most distinctive, there is very little else like them.

SUITABILITY AS HEDGING: Good for mild coastal areas provided it is not too closely clipped.

SITE AND SOIL: Full sun to partial shade in any garden soil if not very heavy or very alkaline. Tolerant of wind and salt spray.

HARDINESS: Fairly hardy.

SPECIAL CARE: No pruning necessary for free-standing shrubs but old or winter-damaged branches should be cut out in spring. Variegated forms can revert to plain green so cut out any all-green shoots. Hedges should be lightly clipped in midsummer. To propagate, take softwood cuttings in summer.

SIZE:: 2 x 1.5m (6½ x 5ft) after five years, ultimately up to 7-8 x 4-5m (23-25 x 13-16ft) in favourable sites.

SIGNIFICANT PROBLEMS

None.

Griselinia littoralis **'Bantry Bay'**

Recommended Varieties

Although the true species is widely available it is worth looking out for variegated forms such as 'Bantry Bay', cream-patterned leaf upper-sides with all-cream lower surfaces; and 'Variegata', white markings on the margins of each leaf, barely hardy, but it is ideal if you can provide extra shelter in a mild garden.

x *Halimiocistus*

**FLOWERING or FRUITING
INTEREST:** Saucer-shaped flowers,
usually white but sometimes with
markings. Each bloom is short-lived
but a succession is produced from early
to midsummer.
FOLIAGE INTEREST: Dark green or
grey green leaves, often downy.
SUITABILITY AS HEDGING: None.
SITE AND SOIL: Sun and a sheltered
position in a well drained soil; a good
choice for sunny banks with dry sandy
soil.
HARDINESS: Fairly hardy.
SPECIAL CARE: Additional feeding
may be needed on light, sandy soils. To
encourage flowering, cut back shoots by
two thirds in late summer but avoid cutting into old wood. To propagate, take
semi-ripe cuttings in summer.
SIZE: 45-60 x 90cm (1½-2 x 3ft).

Recommended Varieties
It's worth looking for these lovely
plants under the name *Cistus* which
many nurseries use. *H. sahucii* (syns.
x *H. revolii*, *Cistus sahucii*) AGM,
downy dark green leaves, white
flowers that may appear intermittently until the autumn, 45 x 90 cm
(1½ x 3ft). *H. wintonensis* (syns.
Cistus wintonensis, *Halimium winto-
nense*) AGM, grey-green leaves,
white flowers with yellow centres
and crimson markings in early summer, 60 x 90cm (2 x 3ft); 'Merrist
Wood Cream' (syn. *Cistus* 'Merrist
Wood Cream') AGM, cream-yellow with dark maroon markings.

SIGNIFICANT PROBLEMS

None.

x Halimiocistus sahucii

Halimium lasianthum (syns. *H. formosum*, *Cistus formosus*, *C. lasianthus*) AGM

**FLOWERING or FRUITING
INTEREST:** Saucer-shaped flowers of
golden yellow with crimson blotches
appear from early to midsummer.
FOLIAGE INTEREST: Small leaves,
often grey-green.
SUITABILITY AS HEDGING: None.
SITE AND SOIL: Sunny sheltered site
with a well drained sandy soil, tolerant of
acidity and alkalinity. Ideal for mild coastal
gardens.
HARDINESS: Barely hardy to fairly
hardy.
SPECIAL CARE: To encourage flowering, cut back shoots by two thirds in
late summer but avoid cutting into old

wood. To propagate, take semi-ripe cuttings in summer.
SIZE: 1 x 1.5m (3 x 5ft).

SIGNIFICANT PROBLEMS
None.

Recommended Varieties
H. 'Susan' AGM, bright yellow
flowers, 45 x 60cm (1½ x 2ft).

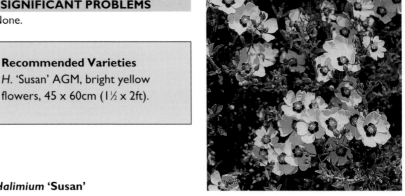

Halimium 'Susan'

SHRUBS

Hebe Shrubby veronica

❝ *Look closely at the individual flower of a hebe and you will under-stand why they are called shrubby veronicas and why they were once part of the speedwell genus. They differ from 'today's' veronicas in their woody, shrubby nature; but are also limited in their distribution to the southern hemisphere, and New Zealand in particular. For this reason, species need to be chosen with care if they are both to beautify northern European summers and survive European winters.* ❞

FLOWERING or FRUITING INTEREST: Not all species flower freely but those that do have white, red, purple or pink flowers in spring or summer and often lasting until the autumn.

FOLIAGE INTEREST: Various leaf sizes and shades of green, grey, silver or bronze depending on the species.

LEFT: *Hebe* 'Autumn Glory'

Hebe cupressoides 'Boughton Dome'

Recommended Varieties

H. 'Autumn Glory', mid-green leaves with red edges, violet flowers from midsummer to late autumn, 60 x 75cm (2-2½ft). *H. buxifolia*, rounded, dark green leaves, white flowers in summer, bushy shrub, 1 x 1.5m (3 x 5ft). *H.* 'Caledonia' (syns. *H.* 'E. B. Anderson', *H.* 'Knightshayes'), pointed leaves with purple red edges, violet flowers from midsummer to late autumn, 60 x 60cm (2 x 2ft). *H.* 'County Park', grey-green leaves with red margins, violet flowers in summer, valuable ground cover, 20 x 45cm (8in x 1½ft). *H. cupressoides* 'Boughton Dome' AGM, grey-green leaves, rarely flowers, dense dome, 60 x 90cm (2 x 3ft). *H.* 'Emerald Green' (syns. *H.* 'Emerald Gem, *H.* 'Green Globe', *H. mackenii*, *H.* 'Milmont Emerald') AGM, bright green leaves, rarely flowers, compact rounded hardy bush, 35 x 50cm (1¼ x 1¾ft). *H. x franciscana* 'Blue Gem' (syn. *H. latifolia*) AGM, light green leaves, deep violet flowers from early summer to mid-autumn, 1.5 x 1.5m (5 x 5ft); *H. x f.* 'Variegata' (syn. *H. elliptica* 'Variegata') AGM, shiny dark green leaves with irregular cream-yellow edges, lilac flowers from midsummer to mid-autumn. *H.* 'Great Orme' AGM, pink flowers that age to white from midsummer to late autumn, erect shrub, 1.5 x 1m (5 x 3ft). *H.* 'Midsummer Beauty' AGM, young leaves is purple, pale violet flowers from midsummer to

SUITABILITY AS HEDGING: Taller species can be used as informal hedging in mild areas.

SITE AND SOIL: Full sun and shelter from cold winds but valuably tolerant of salt spray and wind in mild areas. Any well drained garden soil.

HARDINESS: Varies with species; most are fairly hardy to moderately hardy but variegated types are only barely hardy and in general, the large-leaved types are more tender than the small-leaved forms.

SPECIAL CARE: No pruning is necessary but taller types may be lightly clipped in spring. To propagate, take softwood or semi-ripe cuttings in summer.

SIZE: Varies widely but most attain their ultimate height within five years.

SIGNIFICANT PROBLEMS

Shoot dieback combined with leaf spot, root rot in wet soils, downy mildew.

Hebe pinguifolia 'Pagei'

Hebe rakaiensis

late autumn, bushy shrub, 1.5 x 1m (5 x 3ft). H. 'Mrs Winder' (syn. H. 'Waikiki', H. 'Warleyensis') AGM, bronze-tinted leaves with red-purple edges and young growth is dark purple in winter, violet-blue flowers in autumn, compact shrub, 1 x 1m (3 x 3ft). H. 'Nicola's Blush', leaves have a purple tinge, pink flowers age to white and are produced in two flushes in late spring/early summer and again in autumn, bushy shrub, 75 x 75cm (2½ x 2½ft). H. ochracea 'James Stirling', bronze-green, cypress-like shoots and leaves, sometimes small white flowers, low-growing mound, 40 x 60cm (1½ x 2ft). H. 'Pewter Dome' (syn. H. albicans 'Pewter Dome') AGM, grey-green leaves, white flowers in summer,

rounded bush, 60 x 60cm (2 x 2ft). H. pimeleoides 'Quicksilver' AGM, silver-grey leaves, violet-blue flowers in summer, stiff wiry branches, sprawling habit, 60 x 90cm (2 x 3ft). H. pinguifolia 'Pagei' AGM, small grey-green leaves, small white flowers in spring, valuable ground cover, especially draped over low walls, 20 x 60cm (8in x 2ft). H. rakaiensis AGM, bright green leaves, white spring flowers, dome-shaped and makes a very good low hedge in mild areas as it will withstand light clipping, 90cm x 2m (3 x 6½ft) (a plant whose size is, inexplicably, almost always underestimated). H. 'Red Edge' (syn. H. albicans 'Red Edge') AGM, grey-green leaves with red edges, pale violet-blue flowers in summer, young

growth has a pink tinge in winter, neat spherical bush, 60 x 60cm (2 x 2ft). H. salicifolia, light green leaves, white flowers in midsummer, general experience, including mine, is that this is one of the hardiest forms, 1.5 x 2m (5 x 6½ft). H. topiaria, grey-green leaves, white flowers in summer, neat slow-growing bush, the name indicates that it looks like clipped topiary rather than that it is suitable for it, 75cm x 1m (2½ x 3ft). H. vernicosa, bright shiny green leaves, white flowers from mid-spring to early summer, low-growing and spreading, 30 x 45cm (1 x 1½ft). H. 'Youngii' (syn. H. 'Carl Teschner'), green leaves with red edge, violet-blue flowers in summer, 20 x 60cm (8in x 2ft).

Hypericum St John's wort

❝ *If ever public perception of a genus was conditioned by one species, this is it.* Hypericum *embraces nearly 400 species and a good many hybrids and varieties; yet the southern European* Hypericum calycinum *makes far too many of us imagine that all its relatives are aggressive, shade and drought-tolerant, invasive ground-cover plants too. In truth, they aren't and their relationship to the Rose of Sharon is limited to the form of the flowers. This is a genus ripe for popular investigation.* ❞

FLOWERING or FRUITING INTEREST: Yellow flowers with golden stamens, remarkably consistent in appearance throughout a big genus.

FOLIAGE INTEREST: Grey-green to dark green leaves, some are only evergreen in mild areas.

SUITABILITY AS HEDGING: Forms a fairly rough barrier rather than a hedge.

SITE AND SOIL: Full sun or partial shade in any garden soil. *H. calycinum* can tolerate deep shade and extreme soil conditions such as very dry, acidic or alkaline sites but it can become an invasive weed in the wrong place. Those of borderline hardiness need the protection of a sunny, sheltered wall or fence.

HARDINESS: Moderately hardy.

SPECIAL CARE: Those grown for their leaves should be cut back to soil level in alternate springs. Those grown for their flowers are better pruned annually in spring by cutting back the oldest one third of the shoots to soil level. *H. calycinum* produces suckers and these can be removed from the parent plant or the plant can be divided. To propagate other types, take semi-ripe cuttings in summer or hardwood cuttings in winter. In cold areas, protect the base of the less hardy forms with a winter mulch.

SIZE: Most types attain 30 x 50cm (1 x 1¾ft) after five years, 1 x 1m (3 x 3ft) ultimately.

SIGNIFICANT PROBLEMS
Rust disease on *H. calycinum*.

Hypericum aegypticum

Recommended Varieties
H. aegypticum, mid-green leaves, red tinge to buds, yellow flowers in late summer, semi-evergreen, fairly hardy and a pretty little plant for the rock garden, 50 x 50cm (1¾ x 1¾ft). *H. calycinum*, dark green leaves, yellow flowers from early summer to early autumn, tough evergreen ground cover for dry shade, spreads by underground runners and shouldn't be used in confined areas, individually 45 x 75cm (½ x 2½ft) but more or less indefinitely by suckering. *H. cerastioides* (syn. *H. rhodoppeum*), grey-green leaves, yellow flowers from late spring to early summer, 15 x 40cm (6in x 1½ft). *H.* 'Hidcote' AGM, dark green leaves, large yellow flowers from midsummer to mid-autumn, semi-evergreen, spherical shrub, probably the finest all-round form, 1.2 x 1.2m (4 x 4ft).

Itea ilicifolia Sweetspire

FLOWERING or FRUITING INTEREST: Long delicate fragrant 'catkins' in late summer, which are strictly not catkins but racemes of tiny green-white flowers.

FOLIAGE INTEREST: Glossy dark green leaves.

SUITABILITY AS HEDGING: None.

SITE AND SOIL: Full sun to moderate shade, needs shelter from cold winds so is often grown as a wall shrub. Will grow in most garden soils but best in a moist acidic or neutral soil.

Itea ilicifolia

HARDINESS: Moderately hardy.
SPECIAL CARE: No pruning is
necessary but winter damaged shoots
should be removed in early spring.
Mature plants that are congested will
benefit from having the oldest one-
third of the stems cut out in summer.
To propagate, take semi-ripe cuttings in
summer.
SIZE: 1 x 1m (3 x 3ft) after five years,
ultimately can attain 4 x 3m (13 x 10ft)
in mild areas.

SIGNIFICANT PROBLEMS:
None.

Recommended Varieties
The normal species is the form
usually grown.

Kalmia Calico bush

FLOWERING or FRUITING
INTEREST: Beautiful spherical inflorescences of somewhat rhododendron-like
flowers in shades of pink, red, purple lilac
and white appear in spring.
FOLIAGE INTEREST: Glossy leathery
leaves.
SUITABILITY AS HEDGING: None.
SITE AND SOIL: Full sun to light shade
in a moist acidic soil.
HARDINESS: Fairly hardy to moderately hardy.
SPECIAL CARE: Dead-head flowers
but avoid pruning as the flowers are
borne on old wood. To propagate,
take hardwood cuttings in winter,
K. angustifolia can be layered.
SIZE: Slow-growing attaining 1.5 x 1.5m
(5 x 5ft) after five years, twice this after
15 years.

SIGNIFICANT PROBLEMS:
None.

Recommended Varieties
K. angustifolia rubra, red-purple
flowers in early summer, spreads by
suckers. *K. latifolia* AGM, pink, purple, red or white flowers in early to
midsummer; 'Ostbo Red' AGM, red
buds open to pink flowers.

Kalmia latifolia

Laurus nobilis **Sweet bay, Bay laurel**

❝ *There are several common and popular garden shrubs called laurel and, although this one is now more familiarly called bay, it is in reality the true laurel, with which victors in the Pythian Games of Ancient Greece were garlanded. This is a Mediterranean plant, now more famous as a kitchen herb than a winner's trophy. It has two other interesting attributes: it is extremely expensive to buy once someone has clipped it into a geometric shape (an excellent reason for buying a plant and training it yourself); and it has a remarkable ability to regenerate from old wood; so even if severely killed back in a cold northern winter, it will sprout forth again.* ❞

Laurus nobilis

FLOWERING or FRUITING INTEREST: Yellow-green flowers in early summer.

FOLIAGE INTEREST: Dark green leaves, used as a herb.

SUITABILITY AS HEDGING: Fairly dense hedge for mild areas; individual specimens are very popular for topiary.

SITE AND SOIL: Full sun to deep shade but must have shelter from cold winds or the leaves turn brown. Any garden soil is suitable provided it is not too wet or heavy. Often grown in containers.

HARDINESS: Moderately hardy.

SPECIAL CARE: Pruning is not essential but may be clipped into formal shapes in late spring and late summer. Plants that have been damaged by winter cold should be cut back, into old wood if necessary, in mid-spring.

SIZE: 1.5 x 1.5m (5 x 5ft) after five years, ultimately a tree of 12 x 9m (40 x 30ft) but in practice often grown in a container and clipped to about 1-1.5m (3-5ft) high.

SIGNIFICANT PROBLEMS

Bay sucker, scale insects.

Recommended Varieties

The normal species is the one most frequently grown. There is a pale-leaved variant called 'Aurea' but it is not a true yellow and simply looks unhealthy.

Lavandula angustifolia **Lavender**

FLOWERING or FRUITING INTEREST: Small purple, pink, lavender or white flower spikes appear in summer, most have the familiar perfume.

FOLIAGE INTEREST: Aromatic silver-green leaves.

SUITABILITY AS HEDGING: Some types make excellent low-growing edging, particularly in coastal areas.

SITE AND SOIL: Full sun is essential as is a well drained soil although lavenders will thrive on fairly poor alkaline and stony sites.

HARDINESS: Most of the forms of *L. angustifolia* are hardy but many of the other species are not and will disappoint in cold areas.

SPECIAL CARE: It is worth clipping plants fairly hard after flowers have faded, cutting just into the woody growth. Old plants can be regenerated by cutting back into old wood but it is best to replace them after several years if a neat appearance is important.

SIZE: Low-growing types 60 x 60cm (2 x 2ft) after five years, taller types 1 x 1m (3 x 3ft).

SIGNIFICANT PROBLEMS
Grey mould.

Lavandula angustifolia
'Imperial Gem'

Recommended Varieties

L. angustifolia (syns. *L. officinalis*, *L. spica*) AGM, scented purple-blue flowers from late spring to late summer, low-growing; 'Hidcote' (syn. 'Hidcote Blue') AGM, silver leaves, deep blue flowers in early to midsummer; 'Imperial Gem', grey-green leaves, dark purple flowers, only 30cm (1ft) high; 'Loddon Pink', grey-green leaves, soft pink flowers in midsummer, 45cm (1½ft); 'Nana Alba', grey-green leaves, white flowers in midsummer, only 23cm (9in) high. *L.* x *intermedia* 'Grappenhall', grey-green leaves, only slightly fragrant, lavender flowers, 50 x 80cm (1¾ x 2½ft) with tall flower stems. *L. stoechas* AGM, silver-grey leaves, fragrant dark purple flowers with a tuft of bracts at the tip of the flower head, flowers from late spring to early summer and sometimes again in autumn, hardy but needs good drainage to survive winter, 45cm (1½ft).

Leptospermum Tea tree

FLOWERING or FRUITING INTEREST: Masses of small, usually white, pink or red flowers, from late spring to early summer followed by woody seed capsules.

FOLIAGE INTEREST: Aromatic leaves, colour varies from silver green to dark green depending on the species.

SUITABILITY AS HEDGING: None.

SITE AND SOIL: A warm, sunny site in an acidic or neutral soil; alkaline or dry conditions aren't tolerated. Best suited to mild areas or warm walls but can be grown in a container and moved undercover in winter in cold areas.

HARDINESS: Barely hardy to fairly hardy.

SPECIAL CARE: Pruning not usually necessary. To propagate named varieties, take semi-ripe cuttings in summer; species can be raised from seed.

SIZE: Varies with species.

SIGNIFICANT PROBLEMS
None.

Recommended Varieties

L. rupestre (syns. *L. humifusum*, *L. prostratum*) AGM, dark green leaves, small white flowers, the hardiest species, 30 x 80cm (1 x 2½ft) after five years, ultimately 1 x 1.5m (3 x 5ft). *L. scoparium* 'Kiwi' AGM, red-purple leaves, red flowers, 1 x 1m (3 x 3ft); 'Red Damask' AGM, purple-bronze leaves, double deep red flowers, lax habit, 2 x 1m (6½ x 3ft).

Leptospermum scoparium **'Kiwi'**

SHRUBS

Leucothoe

❝ Among nurserymen's discoveries in recent years has been a group of plants with leaves that I have described as too colourful for their own good. The many-hued water plant Houttuynia cordata *is perhaps the most out-standing example but the appropriately named variety 'Rainbow' of this Oriental member of the* Erica *family is another. I find, however, that while they can be rather attractive on their own, that mixture of colours is very tricky to blend with anything else. And whether there is some obscure connection between having many colours and a need for moisture, I don't know, but the need that this species has for damp conditions is often over-looked and a reason for its failure in many gardens. ❞*

FLOWERING or FRUITING INTEREST: Small white flowers hang down from the stems in early summer.
FOLIAGE INTEREST: Narrow leathery leaves, usually light green but red or purple tints develop in winter.
SUITABILITY AS HEDGING: None.
SITE AND SOIL: Tolerates moderate shade but needs an acidic moist soil with abundant humus. Low-growing arching stems make it ideal for underplanting.
HARDINESS: Very hardy.

SPECIAL CARE: Use an acidic material such as conifer needles when mulching. No pruning necessary but the oldest one-third of the shoots may be cut back to soil level each year to improve the leaves. To propagate, layer or take softwood cuttings in early summer.
SIZE: 60-90cm x 60-90cm (2-3 x 2-3ft) after five years, double this ultimately.

SIGNIFICANT PROBLEMS
None.

Recommended Varieties
L. axillaris 'Scarletta', rich scarlet young growth that turns green, ultimate height 60cm (2ft). *L. walteri* (syn. *L. fontanesiana*) AGM, new growth has red tints, 60 x 60cm (2 x 2ft); 'Rainbow', irregular pink markings that age to cream-white, for best colour grow in light shade.

Ligustrum Privet

FLOWERING or FRUITING INTEREST: Masses of white, spicy-scented flowers in summer.
FOLIAGE INTEREST: Variously coloured or variegated leaves on some varieties.
SUITABILITY AS HEDGING: All of the taller forms make dense and generally very dull hedges but *L. ovalifolium* 'Aureum' is easily the most attractive.
SITE AND SOIL: Full sun to deep shade. Tolerates most garden soils but least reliable on very dry or very wet sites.
HARDINESS: Very hardy although will lose some leaves in very cold winters.
SPECIAL CARE: Clipping in spring will encourage fresh new growth. Those grown as hedges should be clipped two or three times from spring to autumn. To propagate, take semi-ripe cuttings in summer or hardwood cuttings in winter.
SIZE: Without clipping, the taller forms will attain 2 x 1.5m (6 x 5ft) after five years; if clipped 1.5 x 1.2m (5 x 4ft). Ultimate height depends on species.

SIGNIFICANT PROBLEMS
Aphids, honey fungus.

Leucothoe axillaris 'Scarletta'

Recommended Varieties
L. lucidum AGM, oval glossy leaves, cream-white flowers in late summer to early autumn, 1.5 x 1.2m (5 x 4ft) after five years, ultimately 9m (30ft). *L. ovalifolium*, oval mid-green leaves, unpleasantly scented white flowers in midsummer followed by black fruits, trimming removes flowers, 1.5 x 1.2m (5 x 4ft), ultimately 4.5m (14¾ft) tall; 'Aureum' (syn. 'Aureomarginatum') AGM, green leaves with clear golden markings, less vigorous than the species.

Ligustrum ovalifolium 'Aureum'

Lonicera nitida 'Baggesen's Gold' AGM Box-leaved honeysuckle

FLOWERING or FRUITING INTEREST: None but some other shrubby loniceras have scented winter flowers.

FOLIAGE INTEREST: Tiny leaves of golden yellow.

SUITABILITY AS HEDGING: Very good as a dense, brightly coloured hedge.

SITE AND SOIL: Full sun to moderate shade, but the best yellow colour is produced in full sun. Most garden soils are suitable.

HARDINESS: Moderately hardy to hardy.

SPECIAL CARE: No pruning is necessary and it can either be left to form an attractive border shrub or the oldest one-third of the shoots may be cut out each spring. Hedges should be clipped two or three times from mid-spring until mid-autumn. To propagate, take semi-ripe cuttings in summer or hardwood cuttings in winter.

SIZE : 1 x 1.5m (3 x 5ft) in five years, up to 2 x 2m (6½ x 6½ ft) ultimately but can be clipped lower.

SIGNIFICANT PROBLEMS
None.

Recommended Varieties
Apart from *L. nitida* 'Baggesen's Gold' as described above, other good varieties of *Lonicera* include: *L. fragrantissima*, fragrant cream flowers in late winter or early spring, dull red fruits in spring, in exposed sites only semi-evergreen, grows to 2 x 3m (6½ x 10ft). *L. pileata*, green leaves, used as low hedge or ground cover, 1 x 1.5m (3 x 5ft) after five years, ultimately 1.5 x 2m (5 x 6½ft).

Lonicera fragrantissima

Mahonia

❝ *Many plants that flower in winter or early in the spring have yellow flowers. Mahonias are no exceptions but I am constantly saddened that they are seen and appreciated by too few people. Partly this is because the commonest species, the so-called Oregon grape,* Mahonia aquifolium *tends to be planted out of sight, gardeners capitalising on its value as ground cover in shady places. But a contributory factor is that too few of the other, and immeasurably more beautiful, species and varieties are grown because of a widespread belief that they are too tender. They are certainly less hardy than* M. aquifolium, *but given a sheltered position, they could be seen in a great many more gardens than they are now.* ❞

Mahonia aquifolium 'Apollo'

FLOWERING or FRUITING INTEREST: Masses of yellow flowers, often scented, in early spring or late autumn/winter depending on the species. Small grape-like fruits.

FOLIAGE INTEREST: Glossy dull green or purple leaves, often with coloured tints in winter. Each leaf comprises many leaflets, some types are prickly.

SUITABILITY AS HEDGING: None, but *M. aquifolium* will make a low prickly screen.

SITE AND SOIL: Full sun to deep shade. Tolerates most soils but best on deep rich loam.

HARDINESS: Hardy.

SPECIAL CARE: No pruning necessary for *M. aquifolium* but the oldest shoots may with advantage be cut back to soil level every two to three years. The hybrid mahonias can be made more compact by cutting back the non-flowering shoots by about half in mid-spring. Mahonias are difficult to root from cuttings so try layering.

SIZE: Varies greatly depending on the species.

SIGNIFICANT PROBLEMS

Rust on *M. aquifolium* can be extremely disfiguring and difficult to control.

Mahonia x media 'Lionel Fortescue'

Myrtus communis AGM Myrtle

FLOWERING or FRUITING INTEREST: Sweetly-scented white flowers with prominent stamens appear in summer sometimes followed by black-purple fruits.

FOLIAGE INTEREST: Glossy dark green leaves, aromatic when crushed.

SUITABILITY AS HEDGING: None except in very mild areas where it can be used to form a low edging.

SITE AND SOIL: Full sun to moderate shade, needs a warm sheltered site. Tolerates most soils except cold wet sites. Can be grown in a container in cold areas and taken under cover in winter.

HARDINESS: Fairly hardy to moderately hardy.

SPECIAL CARE: No pruning necessary but frost-damaged shoots should be cut out in spring and plants with formal outlines be clipped in early summer. To propagate, take semi-ripe cuttings in summer.

SIZE: 1 x 1m (3 x 3ft) within five years, ultimately 5 x 3m (16 x 10ft).

SIGNIFICANT PROBLEMS
None.

Myrtus communis tarentina

Olearia Daisy bush

❝ *I always find there is something specially rewarding about finding flowers of a particular form in an unexpected place. And so it is with daisies. Although the daisy family is one of the largest in the plant world and its species span almost every possible life form, it's an inescapable fact that in temperate climates, you expect to see daisies on herbaceous plants. So finding them on a shrub is satisfying; and when it is as handsome as one of the Australasian tree daisies in the genus* Olearia, *it is especially so. Like so many other very beautiful evergreens, (and indeed so many from New Zealand), it isn't as hardy as might be wished; but then you can't have absolutely everything.* ❞

FLOWERING or FRUITING INTEREST: Profusion of small daisy-like flowers in early summer.
FOLIAGE INTEREST: Leathery mid-green leaves with white undersides.
SUITABILITY AS HEDGING: Good hedging in mild coastal gardens.
SITE AND SOIL: A warm sunny site is necessary, in cold areas they need a sunny, sheltered wall or fence. In mild areas they can tolerate winds and salt spray. Most garden soils are suitable, including alkaline conditions provided they are well drained.
HARDINESS: Fairly hardy.
SPECIAL CARE: Cut out the oldest one third of the stems in midsummer after flowering. Any straggly growth should be cut out in spring. To propagate, take semi-ripe cuttings in late summer or hardwood cuttings in autumn.
SIZE: 1 x 1m (3 x 3ft) after five years, the eventual size varying with the species.

> **Recommended Varieties**
> *O. macrodonta* AGM, holly-like leaves, papery bark, tiny white flowers in early summer, the whole plant has musky odour, large upright shrub, ultimately 4m (13ft) tall.
> *O. nummulariifolia*, small, leathery yellow-green leaves, small fragrant white flowers in midsummer, one of the hardiest species, spherical bush, ultimately 3m (10ft) tall. *O. solandri*, scented pale yellow flowers in late summer, needs wall protection, heath-like shrub, 2 x 2m (6 x 6ft).

SIGNIFICANT PROBLEMS

None.

Osmanthus

FLOWERING or FRUITING INTEREST: Scented masses of small tubular white flowers. Small black-purple fruits.
FOLIAGE INTEREST: Glossy leathery leaves in various colours.
SUITABILITY AS HEDGING: None.
SITE AND SOIL: Best in light shade or sun. Most gardens soils are suitable, including alkaline sites, but intolerant of very heavy or wet conditions.
HARDINESS: Very hardy.
SPECIAL CARE: No pruning is necessary but long growths should be shortened in spring. To propagate, take semi-ripe cuttings in late summer.
SIZE: Most 1 x 1m (3 x 3ft) after five years, most are 4 x 4m (13 x 13ft) ultimately but some forms are smaller.

Olearia nummulariifolia

Osmanthus x burkwoodii

SIGNIFICANT PROBLEMS

None.

Ozothamnus rosmarinifolius
'Silver Jubilee'

Recommended Varieties

O. x *burkwoodii* (syn. x *Osmarea burkwoodii*) AGM, glossy dark green leaves with silver undersides, scented small white flowers in spring, dense shrub, 1m x 60cm (3 x 2ft) after five years, ultimately 3 x 3m (10 x 10ft). *O. delavayi* AGM, glossy dark green leaves,. fragrant long white flowers in mid- to late spring, blue-black fruits in autumn, 60 x 60cm (2 x 2ft) after five years, double this ultimately. *O. heterophyllus* (syn. *O. ilicifolius*), spiny holly-like dark green leaves, small inflorescences of scented white flowers in autumn, purple-black fruits in early winter; 'Goshiki' (syn. 'Tricolor'), spiny, young growth bronze, later leaves heavily mottled with cream-yellow and green; 'Variegatus' (syn. 'Argenteomarginatus') AGM, cream-white leaf edges, few flowers.

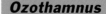

Ozothamnus

FLOWERING or FRUITING INTEREST: Masses of small flowers in summer with a spicy perfume.
FOLIAGE INTEREST: Dense, needle-like, dull green leaves.
SUITABILITY AS HEDGING: None.
SITE AND SOIL: Full sun to light shade. Plant in a warm sheltered position to capture the perfume. Tolerates most garden soils except very heavy wet sites.
HARDINESS: Fairly hardy to moderately hardy.
SPECIAL CARE:
 No pruning necessary. To propagate, take semi-ripe cuttings in summer.
SIZE: Varies greatly with the species.

SIGNIFICANT PROBLEMS

None.

Recommended Varieties

O. ledifolius, sticky leaves giving off an inflammable vapour, yellow undersides to leaves, red flower buds in late spring, yellow-white flowers tinged with red in early summer, 50 x 40cm (1¾ x 1½ft) after five years, ultimately 80cm (2½ft) tall. *O. rosmarinifolius*, leaves like that of rosemary, white hairs on branches, purple or pink in bud, white flowers in summer, erect habit, 1.8 x 1.2 m (5¾ x 4ft) after five years, ultimately 3m (10ft); 'Silver Jubilee' AGM, white felt-like branches, silver leaves, pink buds, white flowers, a superb form with more flowers than you would have thought possible.

Pachysandra terminalis AGM

" *My first encounter with* Pachysandra *was very many years ago when a friend brought me a characteristically toothed leaf and asked for an identification. I immediately showed it to an ancient head gardener who told me it was the finest herbaceous ground cover that he knew. Like much of his wisdom, the remarks stuck with me until I had need of just such a ground cover for a shady place in my own garden. I planted* Pachysandra *and was bitterly disappointed, as it grew feebly and certainly didn't cover much ground. Since then, I have learned more about this plant and wouldn't again try it, as I did then, in a dry light soil. Give it the conditions that it needs and my old Head Gardener chum will be proved correct; as, eventually, he usually is.* "

Pachysandra terminalis

FLOWERING or FRUITING INTEREST: Small white flowers in late spring; sometimes white fruits.

FOLIAGE INTEREST: Dark green toothed leaves.

SUITABILITY AS HEDGING: None.

SITE AND SOIL: Can tolerate moderate to deep shade. Will grow in most soils even if dry, but best in deep, moist ground enriched with leaf mould. Avoid shallow alkaline sites. A good ground cover beneath shrubs.

HARDINESS: Very hardy.

SPECIAL CARE : To propagate, divide in spring or autumn.

SIZE : 20 x 30-45cm (8in x 1-1½ft).

SIGNIFICANT PROBLEMS:
None.

Recommended Varieties
The normal species is the form usually planted; there is a variegated variety *P. t.* 'Variegata' AGM which is much slower growing and rarely flowers but has attractive green leaves edged with cream.

Phillyrea angustifolia   Jasmine box

FLOWERING or FRUITING INTEREST: Fragrant tiny cream flowers are borne in clusters from late spring to early summer.

FOLIAGE INTEREST: Dark green or yellow grey-green leaves that are narrow and lance-shaped, like those of the olive tree.

SUITABILITY AS HEDGING: Suitable for an informal hedge.

SITE AND SOIL: Sun or partial shade in any fairly good garden soil. Tolerant of hot dry conditions and salt spray and a good plant therefore for coastal gardens.

HARDINESS: Moderately hardy to hardy.

SPECIAL CARE: Dense twiggy growth does not need routine pruning but cut back any winter-damaged shoots into the old wood in spring. To propagate take semi-ripe cuttings in early summer.

SIZE: 2 x 2m (6½ x 6½ft) after 10 years, ultimately 3m (10ft) tall.

SIGNIFICANT PROBLEMS
None.

Phillyrea angustifolia

Recommended Varieties
The normal species is usually grown.

Photinia

**FLOWERING or FRUITING
INTEREST:** *P. davidiana* has small white
flowers in spring followed by red fruits.
FOLIAGE INTEREST: Intense red
colour on young shoots in spring.
SUITABILITY AS HEDGING: In
mild areas may be used as an informal
hedge.
SITE AND SOIL: Light to moderate
shade. A sheltered site will protect the
tender new leaves from late frosts.
Any garden soil is suitable but thrives
best on a slightly acidic loam with abundant humus.
HARDINESS: Moderately hardy.
SPECIAL CARE : No pruning necessary but misshapen plants should be
cut back in spring and will regenerate.
Hedges may be clipped lightly in early
summer. To propagate, take semi-ripe
cuttings in summer.
SIZE: 1.5 x 2m (5 x 6½ft) after five years
and 4 x 4m (13 x 13ft) ultimately.

SIGNIFICANT PROBLEMS
None.

Photinia davidiana **'Red Robin'**

Recommended Varieties
P. davidiana (syn. *Stranvaesia
davidiana*), semi-evergreen, dark
green leaves turns orange/red and
falls in early winter, flowers and red
fruits, a larger shrub at 2.4 x 2.4 m
(6¾ x 6¾ft); 'Palette', a variegated
form with blotches and streaks
of cream-white and pink tints.
P. x fraseri 'Red Robin' AGM, vivid
red growth early in the season,
later mellowing to red-bronze. *P.*
'Redstart' AGM, red young growth
later turns green.

Phyllodoce empetriformis Mountain heather, Blue heather

**FLOWERING or FRUITING
INTEREST:** Small bell-shaped rose-red
flowers from mid-spring to midsummer.
FOLIAGE INTEREST: small narrow
bright green leaves.
SUITABILITY AS HEDGING: None.
SITE AND SOIL: Partial shade in an
acidic soil enriched with humus. Needs
protection against cold drying winds
and strong sun. Best grown in an acid
soil bed or rock garden.
HARDINESS: Very hardy.
SPECIAL CARE: Plants should be
trimmed into shape after flowering. To
propagate, take semi-ripe heeled cuttings
in midsummer. Plants are hardy but in
their native habitat are covered with a
blanket of snow over winter; in gardens
cover them with conifer trimmings or
similar winter protection.

SIZE: 15 x 20cm (6 x 8in) after five
years, ultimately 25cm (10in).

SIGNIFICANT PROBLEMS
None.

Recommended Varieties
The true species is the form
normally grown.

Pieris

"Many garden shrubs are chosen for the appeal of the change in their leaf colour during the season. Almost all are deciduous species whose green foliage becomes yellow, red or orange before dropping in the autumn. With very few exceptions, this autumnal colour change doesn't occur with evergreens whose leaves fall piecemeal. But pay attention to the other end of the season and you will find a few species offering a colour change then, the new shoots appearing in one hue to alter to another as summer progresses. And none is better at this than Pieris. *"*

FLOWERING or FRUITING INTEREST: Large hanging inflorescences of small cream or pink flowers in spring.
FOLIAGE INTEREST: Leathery dark green leaves with vivid red young growth in spring.
SUITABILITY AS HEDGING: None.

SITE AND SOIL: A sheltered site in light to moderate shade. The soil must be acidic and enriched with humus to provide a moist but well-drained environment.
HARDINESS: Moderately hardy.
SPECIAL CARE: Use acidic mulch such as conifer needles. No pruning is necessary. To propagate, take semi-ripe cuttings in summer or layer.
SIZE: 50 x 75cm (1¾ x 2½ft) after five years, 2 x 2m (6½ x 6½ft) or more ultimately.

SIGNIFICANT PROBLEMS
None.

LEFT: *Pieris formosa* **'Wakehurst'**
BELOW: *Pieris japonica* **'Little Heath'**

Recommended Varieties
It's important to decide if your main preference is for flowers or leaves and then choose accordingly.

P. 'Flaming Silver' AGM, vivid red young growth, silver-white margin to the leaves, cream-white flowers, small shrub. P. 'Forest Flame' AGM, best for leaves, vivid red young growth fades to pink or cream then turns green, rarely flowers, large shrub.
P. formosa var. forrestii 'Wakehurst' AGM, bright red young growth fading to pink then green, white flowers, light overhead shade will offer protection from frosts. P. japonica 'Little Heath' AGM, yellow-green variegated leaves, pink buds, sparse flowers, compact with small leaves; 'Mountain Fire' AGM, deep red new growth ageing to glossy brown, white flowers; 'Variegata', white variegated leaves, white flowers, slow-growing.

Pittosporum tenuifolium

FLOWERING or FRUITING INTEREST:
Some forms have small, rather fragrant flowers.
FOLIAGE INTEREST: Small oval grey-green leaves with wavy edges. Often prettily variegated or with contrasting dark stems.
SUITABILITY AS HEDGING: In mild areas it can make an informal screen or be planted as part of a mixed hedge.
SITE AND SOIL: Full sun or light

shade with shelter from cold winds. An ideal plant for mild coastal sites; in other areas often grown against a warm wall or fence or grown in containers. Tolerates most garden soils but not successful on very alkaline sites.

HARDINESS: Fairly hardy to moderately hardy.

SPECIAL CARE: In cold areas, protect young plants over winter. *P. tenuifolium* will re-grow from old wood so winter damage should be cut out in spring. No regular pruning is necessary but hedges should be clipped twice a year in midsummer and early autumn. To propagate, take semi-ripe cuttings in late summer.

SIZE: 1.5-2 x 1m (5-6½x 3ft) after five years, about 6 x 2.5-3m (20 x 8-10ft) ultimately in mild areas.

SIGNIFICANT PROBLEMS
None.

Recommended Varieties
P. 'Garnettii' AGM, grey-green leaves with white leaf margins and in winter pink-purple spots, large shrub, hermaphrodite, overall probably the best and most reliable form. You will still sometimes see it listed as a variety of the following species. *P. tenuifolium* AGM, dark branches with various coloured leaves, fragrant dark red flowers in spring, grow as hedge or large shrub; 'Silver Queen' AGM, pale silver-grey leaves with white wavy edges, dark red flowers in spring, pyramid-shaped tree; 'Tom Thumb' AGM, pale green leaves becoming dark purple over winter, dark red flowers with yellow anthers, dwarf spherical shrub 1m (3ft) tall. *P. tobira* AGM, mid-green leaves, scented cream-white flowers in summer followed by yellow seed capsules, barely hardy and only successful in mild gardens.

Polygala chamaebuxus AGM

FLOWERING or FRUITING INTEREST:
Clusters of flowers with yellow or white lips and bright yellow wings appear late spring to early summer.

FOLIAGE INTEREST: Glossy dark green oval leaves.

SUITABILITY AS HEDGING: None.

SITE AND SOIL: Partial shade in an acidic or neutral soil. Ideal for woodland conditions or under shrubs.

HARDINESS: Very hardy.

SPECIAL CARE: Mulch with acidic material such as conifer needles. No pruning necessary. To propagate, take softwood heeled cuttings in early summer, layer or sow seed in autumn.

SIZE: 15 x 30cm (6in x 1ft) after five years, ultimately will spread to 1m (3ft).

SIGNIFICANT PROBLEMS
None.

LEFT: *Pittosporum* 'Garnettii'
RIGHT: *Polygala chamaebuxus* var. *grandiflora*

Recommended Varieties
More colourful then the species is *P. c.* var. *grandiflora* (syns. 'Purpurea', 'Rhodoptera') AGM, large flowers with bright yellow lips, deep rose-purple wings.

SHRUBS

Prunus laurocerasus AGM Cherry Laurel

❝I mentioned on page 48 that several garden shrubs are called laurel. Ironically, the one to which the name is most frequently applied is this species, which isn't a true laurel; not a Laurus, but a Prunus. In some ways, it's also the plant that has given laurels and indeed all broad-leaved evergreen plants something of a bad name. For the cherry laurel was the great dark, forbidding plant of Victorian Rectory gardens, a sombre hedge that attracted both soot and sooty mould and was awesome to clip. This is a pity for, undeniably, it still has its uses: it is fairly quick growing, it is ultimately fairly dense, it is tough, will grow almost anywhere; and it is relatively inexpensive. ❞

FLOWERING or FRUITING INTEREST: Clusters of small white flowers in spring followed by black fruits in early autumn.

FOLIAGE INTEREST: Large oval glossy green leaves.

SUITABILITY AS HEDGING: Excellent large dense hedge or windbreak.

SITE AND SOIL: Full sun to deep shade. Thrives well on almost any garden soil and tolerant of fairly alkaline conditions, despite popular belief to the contrary.

HARDINESS: Very hardy.

SPECIAL CARE: No pruning necessary, but can be clipped in midsummer and again in early autumn. It is a laborious task however as if done with shears rather than secateurs, the large leaves are sliced and turn brown and unsightly.

SIZE: 3 x 3m (10 x 10ft) after five years, 7-8 x 5m (23-25 x 16ft) ultimately.

SIGNIFICANT PROBLEMS
None.

Prunus laurocerasus 'Otto Luyken'

> **Recommended Varieties**
> *P. l.* 'Otto Luyken' AGM has a low-growing, spreading habit, 1 x 1m (3 x 3ft) and the best flowers although it isn't big enough for a hedge, for which purpose the basic species remains your choice.

Pyracantha Firethorn

FLOWERING or FRUITING INTEREST: Clusters of tiny white flowers in early summer. Long-lasting fruits in red, orange or yellow depending on the variety.

FOLIAGE INTEREST: Mid- to dark green leaves, sharp thorns.

SUITABILITY AS HEDGING: Excellent thorny hedges.

SITE AND SOIL: Full sun to moderate shade, ideal for cool walls. Any fairly good garden soil but leaves exhibits yellowing on alkaline sites.

HARDINESS: Very hardy.

SPECIAL CARE: Those grown as wall shrubs can be grown informally or trained formally into an espalier or fan. For the best display of fruits on established plants, shorten all new side-shoots in midsummer so that only three leaves remain. Free-standing specimens don't require annual pruning but may be cut back hard in late winter to control them. To propagate, take semi-ripe cuttings in late summer.

SIZE: 1.5 x 1.5m (5 x 5ft) after five years, 4 x 4m (13 x 13ft) ultimately.

SIGNIFICANT PROBLEMS
Aphids, fireblight, scab. Birds will also strip the fruits.

FAR LEFT: *Pyracantha coccinea* 'Red Column' LEFT: *Pyracantha coccinea* 'Orange Glow'

Rhamnus alaternus 'Argenteovariegata' AGM Buckthorn

FLOWERING or FRUITING INTEREST: Small green-white flowers in summer sometimes followed by red fruits ripening to black (poisonous) in autumn.

FOLIAGE INTEREST: Variegated grey-green leaves with cream margins.

SUITABILITY AS HEDGING: Excellent in very mild areas.

SITE AND SOIL: Full sun or partial shade, suitable for any garden soil including alkaline sites. Tolerant of pollution and salt spray.

HARDINESS: Barely hardy to fairly hardy; this lovely variegated form is slightly less hardy than the true species.

SPECIAL CARE: Protect young plants over winter. No pruning necessary but it may be clipped into shape in midsummer.

To propagate, take semi-ripe cuttings in late summer or hardwood cuttings in autumn.

SIZE: 1 x 1m (3 x 3ft) after five years, ultimately can attain 4m (13ft).

SIGNIFICANT PROBLEMS
None.

Rhamnus alaternus 'Argenteovariegata'

Rhododendron

"This must be one of, if not the, most immediately recognisable shrub genus of them all. With rather few exceptions (and mostly among non-hardy species), the flowers of rhododendrons are relatively uniform, and their foliage even more so. The individual leaves do vary, in size, in relatively glossiness and in the relative presence of a hairy indumentum; but a Rhododendron *leaf is always a* Rhododendron *leaf. Those I have selected here should be both attractive and reliable in most parts of the country; sadly, its relative tenderness obliges me to excuse* R. sinogrande, *its huge leaves being among the largest of any garden plant.* "*

RIGHT: *Rhododendron 'Britannia'*
BELOW: *R. campylocarpum*

FLOWERING or FRUITING INTEREST: Large inflorescences of beautiful spring flowers in various colours depending on the variety.

FOLIAGE INTEREST: Medium to large glossy green leaves with more or less of a felt-like indumentum on the undersides.

SUITABILITY AS HEDGING: May be used to form a large informal screen; the much maligned *R. ponticum* achieves this very successfully in large woodland gardens. But always remember that they are intolerant of clipping.

SITE AND SOIL: Light to moderate shade is preferred to prevent frost or wind damage to the flowers and young leaves; a few types tolerate full sun. Best in acidic soil that is enriched with humus so the conditions are moist but not water-logged. Quite intolerant of any alkalinity or dryness.

HARDINESS: Varies from fairly hardy to very hardy. Most are moderately hardy.

SPECIAL CARE: The root-ball should be covered by no more than 3cm (1in) of soil. Use an acidic material such as conifer needles when mulching. If the size of the plant permits, pull off dead flowerheads using finger and thumb, but take care not to remove the buds that will form next

year's flowers. Layering plants is the easiest way to propagate them as they are unreliable from cuttings.

SIZE: Varies greatly depending on species or variety. Dwarf forms are between 1-3 x 1-2m (3-10 x 3-6½ft); large types are small tree sized.

For rhododendrons the problems are leaf spots, powdery mildew, bud blast, vine weevil. With azaleas the problems include rabbits, deer and galls.

Rhododendron 'Hinomayo'

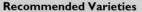

Recommended Varieties
There are many hundreds of varieties available that vary rather little in their leaf appeal and in any event, few gardeners will choose rhododendrons on leaf appeal alone. The smaller hardier types are best for most gardens.

Species
R. campylocarpum, glossy green leaves with glaucous green undersides, bell-shaped clear yellow flowers, may take several years before flowering, hardy, medium-sized shrub. *R. impeditum*, tiny coarse leaves, masses of funnel-shaped light blue-mauve flowers, dwarf alpine shrub for the rock garden. *R. pemakoense*, small leaves, funnel-shaped pink-purple flowers, buds prone to frost damage, very compact dwarf only a few centimetres high. *R. ponticum*, purple flowers, large shrub, naturalised and now considered a weed in many areas but, given space, it still has its uses. *R.*

yakushimanum (syn. *R. degronianum* ssp. *yakushimanum*), narrow dark green leaves with red-brown indumentum, rose-pink in bud, pink flowers that fade to white, very hardy, suitable for sun or shade, a small dome-shaped species up to 1 x 1.2 m (3 x 4ft) and immeasurably better than most of the hybrids derived from it.

Hybrids
Blue Tit Group, inflorescences of small blue-mauve flowers, hardy, 1 x 1m (3 x 3ft). Bow Bells Group, copper-coloured young growth, cerise in bud, bell-shaped pink flowers, hardy, 1m (3ft). 'Britannia', crimson-scarlet flowers, more tolerant than most of strong winds, hardy, slow-growing but ultimately large rounded bush, 3m (10ft). 'Chikor', small leaves, yellow flowers, hardy, twiggy dwarf, 1m (3ft). 'Dora Amateis' AGM, small dull green leaves, pale pink buds, white flowers lightly spotted with yellow, very

hardy, semi-dwarf, mound-forming shrub. Elizabeth Group, mid-green leaves, susceptible to mildew, dark red flowers in spring and again in autumn, dome-shaped, 1.5m (5ft). 'Pink Pearl', rose-pink buds, large pink flowers with brown speckling, vigorous shrub, can be straggly in the shade, hardy, tall, over 3.5m (12ft).

Evergreen azaleas
The following varieties are sometimes called Japanese azaleas. They can withstand hotter, drier sites than dwarf rhododendrons. Plant in full sun in cool areas or light shade in mild areas.
'Addy Wery' AGM, early scarlet flowers, hardy, upright habit. 'Hinode-giri' early bright crimson flowers, hardy, low to medium habit. 'Hinomayo' AGM, bright pink flowers, lower than most, up to 1.5m (5ft), hardy, almost deciduous. 'Vuyk's Scarlet' AGM, early crimson flowers with wavy petals, hardy, a good choice for cool gardens.

SHRUBS

Ribes speciosum AGM Fuchsia-flowered gooseberry

❝There are some garden plants that individual gardeners take to their hearts; and sometimes quite inexplicably so. This is one that I have adored and admired since I first saw it growing in one of those mild, damp, acidic west of Scotland gardens. It is, in some ways, like a fuchsia but it certainly isn't a fuchsia; and nor, most assuredly, is it a gooseberry. It has an individual and silent brooding beauty that I love. Yet I have met other gardeners who are totally at a loss to understand my passion; especially as my garden soil and climate don't even permit me to grow it myself.❞

FLOWERING or FRUITING INTEREST: Deep red flowers, rather like those of a species *Fuchsia*, hang down in clusters during mid- to late spring.
FOLIAGE INTEREST: Semi-evergreen with red bristly stems and shiny green leaves.
SUITABILITY AS HEDGING: None.
SITE AND SOIL: Light shade. A slightly acidic soil is preferred which should be moist yet free-draining. In cold areas, should be grown against a warm wall or fence.
HARDINESS: Barely hardy to fairly hardy.
SPECIAL CARE: No pruning is necessary apart from cutting out frost damaged branches. To propagate, take semi-ripe cuttings in summer or hardwood cuttings in winter.
SIZE: 1 x 1m (3 x 3ft) after five years, 2.5 x 2.5m (8 x 8ft) ultimately.

SIGNIFICANT PROBLEMS
Aphids.

Recommended Varieties
The true species is the only form available.

Rosmarinus officinalis Rosemary

FLOWERING or FRUITING INTEREST: Small inflorescences, usually blue, mauve or pink, appear from mid-spring to early summer.
FOLIAGE INTEREST: Small needle-like blue-green leaves, aromatic, widely used as a herb.
SUITABILITY AS HEDGING: The more upright growing forms such as 'Miss Jessopp's Upright' make very good informal medium-sized hedges as they will tolerate close clipping.
SITE AND SOIL: Thrives in full sun and a well drained soil but can tolerate light shade. Avoid water-logged sites or those with extremes of pH.
HARDINESS: Fairly hardy to moderately hardy depending on variety; the dark blue forms are generally the more tender.
SPECIAL CARE: Cut out the oldest one-third of the shoots in spring to avoid

Ribes speciosum

Rosmarinus officinalis **'Majorca Pink'**

the plant becoming woody and leggy. Hedges should clipped twice during the growing season, once in midsummer and again in early autumn. To propagate, take semi-ripe cuttings in summer.

SIZE: The larger forms will attain their maximum height of 1.5-2m (5-6½ft) within five years, but sizes and shapes vary widely with variety.

Recommended Varieties

The basic species is a good plant but other forms offer a range of habits, flower colour and hardiness: *R. o.* var. *albiflorus*, white flowers; 'Majorca Pink', dull green leaves, lilac-pink flowers from early spring, moderately hardy, columnar habit, 1.2m (4ft); 'Miss Jessopp's Upright' (syns. 'Fastigiatus', f. *pyramidalis*) AGM, light mauve-blue flowers, vigorous erect habit, good for hedging, 1m (3ft) after five years, ultimately 2m (6½ft); 'Prostratus Group' (syns. *R. corsicus* 'Prostratus', *R. x lavandulaceus, R. officinalis* var. *lavandulaceus, R. o.* var. *repens, R. repens*) AGM, light blue flowers, barely to fairly hardy, prostrate forming large dense mats up to 60cm (2ft); 'Severn Sea' AGM, violet-blue flowers, only fairly hardy, spreading arching habit up to 1m (3ft) tall.

Rubus tricolor

FLOWERING or FRUITING INTEREST: Sparse single white flowers in summer. Sometimes red raspberry-like fruits appear.

FOLIAGE INTEREST: Semi-evergreen, heart-shaped dark green leaves with red tints and white undersides. The stems are covered in red bristles.

SUITABILITY AS HEDGING: None.

SITE AND SOIL: Full sun to moderate shade. Most garden soils are tolerated provided they are not water-logged. The long trailing stems root readily, so position carefully or the plant will be invasive; but, by the same token, it provides good ground cover in otherwise inhospitable places.

HARDINESS: Very hardy but leaves will be browned by very cold winds.

SPECIAL CARE: Feed with a balanced general fertiliser in spring. If grown in the wilder parts of a garden it should be left unpruned, otherwise cut back to the crown each spring to encourage new growth.

SIZE: 75cm x 1.5m (2½ x 5ft) (individual plants) after five years, double this spread ultimately.

Recommended Varieties

The true species is the one normally available, selected forms may be offered that claim to be more reliably evergreen.

Rubus tricolor

Ruscus aculeatus Butcher's Broom

" Strictly, this is a leafless evergreen for the 'leaves' are in reality flattened stems; but you would never know it. The shrub has a reputation for being dull and boring; in truth, the female plants in fruit are rather pretty and there's no denying that it will grow in places that almost nothing else will. "

FLOWERING or FRUITING INTEREST: Tiny green flowers in spring or autumn. Fertilised female plants produce red fruits in autumn that last well into the winter.

FOLIAGE INTEREST: Small pointed 'leaves' are modified stems called cladodes.

SUITABILITY AS HEDGING: Not very effective although a double row, closely planted will form an informal screen.

SITE AND SOIL: Moderate to deep shade. Will grow in almost any soil, even if very dry.

HARDINESS: Very hardy

SPECIAL CARE: No pruning necessary. To propagate, remove suckers or divide in spring.

SIZE: 50 x 50cm (1¾ x 1¾ft) in five years and 1.2 x 1m (4 x 3ft) ultimately.

SIGNIFICANT PROBLEMS
None.

> **Recommended Varieties**
> The normal species will be the form most likely to be seen but the sexes are borne on separate plants and both are needed for fruits to develop on females. A hermaphrodite form is available from specialist nurseries and this circumvents the problem.

Ruscus aculeatus

Ruta graveolens Rue

FLOWERING or FRUITING INTEREST: Clusters of small yellow flowers in summer.

FOLIAGE INTEREST: Finely-divided blue-green leaves, aromatic when crushed. Some people are allergic to the leaves so wear gloves when handling.

SUITABILITY AS HEDGING: None.

SITE AND SOIL: Full sun, tolerates most garden soils including poor alkaline sites if they are well drained.

HARDINESS: Moderately hardy to hardy.

SPECIAL CARE: The young growth has the best coloured leaves so remove two or three shoots to soil level each spring to encourage this. Trim lightly in early summer. To propagate, take semi-ripe cuttings in summer.

SIZE: 75 x 60cm (2½ x 2ft) after two years.

SIGNIFICANT PROBLEMS
None.

> **Recommended Varieties**
> The normal species is widely available but a better foliage plant is *R. g.* 'Jackman's Blue' AGM, which has particularly vivid blue leaves and a more compact shape but flowers less reliably.

Ruta graveolens 'Jackman's Blue'

Santolina Cotton lavender

**FLOWERING or FRUITING
INTEREST:** Small button-like yellow
flowers in summer.

FOLIAGE INTEREST: Very tiny
green or silver leaves.

SUITABILITY AS HEDGING: Good
low edging, often clipped for formal effect
around herb gardens.

SITE AND SOIL: Full sun and a light
free-draining soil are essential.

HARDINESS: Moderately hardy to
hardy.

SPECIAL CARE: Lightly trim the
plants in late spring, cutting just above
the base of the previous season's growth
and trim again after flowering. Edging
plants should be sheared into shape
once a year after flowering. To propagate,
take semi-ripe cuttings in late summer.

SIZE: If not clipped, will attain its full
height of 50 x 75cm (1¾ x 2½ft) within
five years when they will inevitably
become leggy and are best replaced.

SIGNIFICANT PROBLEMS
None.

Santolina chamaecyparissus
'Lambrook Silver'

Recommended Varieties
S. chamaecyparissus (syn. *S. incana*)
AGM is the normal species offered
but there are also selected forms,
such as 'Lambrook Silver' which has
the best silver leaves and a neat
habit. *S. pinnata* spp. *neapolitana*
'Edward Bowles', feathery grey-
green leaves, pale primrose flowers.

Skimmia

**FLOWERING or FRUITING
INTEREST:** Small white-yellow flowers
in spring. Some have very attractive red-
pink buds over winter. Female plants
produce rich red fruits that persist
throughout the winter.

FOLIAGE INTEREST: Leathery
aromatic dark green leaves.

SUITABILITY AS HEDGING: None.

SITE AND SOIL: Light to moderate
shade, the leaves will yellow in sun.
The ideal soil is moist and organic; leaves
will turn yellow and shoots die back
on water-logged, dry, shallow or alkaline
sites. Tolerant of salt spray and pollution.

HARDINESS: Hardy.

SPECIAL CARE: No pruning is necessary but old plants will regenerate if
the oldest one third of the shoots are
cut back to soil level in spring. To propagate, take semi-ripe cuttings in summer
or hardwood cuttings in winter.

SIZE: Most will attain 60 x 60cm
(2 x 2ft) after five years and ultimately
1-1.2m (3-4ft).

SIGNIFICANT PROBLEMS
None.

Skimmia japonica reevesiana

Recommended Varieties
S. x confusa 'Kew Green' AGM,
male, rich green leaves, aromatic
when crushed, sweet-scented
cream flowers, tolerates full sun,
45 x 60cm (1½ x 2ft) ultimately
1m (3ft). *S. japonica*, female and
produces bright red fruits if a male
plant is nearby, pale to mid-green
leaves, small white flowers in
spring; 'Nymans' AGM, female, red
stalks, free-fruiting; spp. *reevesiana*,
hermaphrodite, dark green leaves,
cream-white flowers in late spring,
deep red fruits in late summer,
compact, 75 x 75cm (2½ x 2½ft);
'Rubella' AGM, male, bright green
leaves with red rims, copper-
coloured stalks, pink buds all
winter, scented flowers in early
spring, 1.5 x 1.5m (5 x 5ft).

Ulex europaeus Gorse

❝ *Like* Ruscus *(page 66), this is another plant that, in a strict, botanical sense, is all but devoid of leaves. But here they are reduced to spines and the green shoots help to reinforce the illusion. I'm always surprised that gorse hasn't made more of an impact in gardens. I accept that it has a lax, rather unkempt habit that certainly wouldn't be appropriate in a small space. But seen in flower in its native habitat, it is utterly spectacular and in larger, wilder gardens with suitable soil, it (and its double flowered form especially) can similarly be eye-catching. It also makes one of the most impenetrable barriers imaginable; it is a determined intruder indeed who will wade through a few metres of boundary gorse planting.* ❞

FLOWERING or FRUITING INTEREST: Honey-scented pea-like yellow flowers from early to late spring and then intermittently throughout the year.

FOLIAGE INTEREST: Mid- to dark green shoots and sharp spines give the 'foliage' appeal as these shrubs are almost leafless.

SUITABILITY AS HEDGING: Can be grown as low informal and impenetrable hedge.

SITE AND SOIL:
Full sun in a poor soil that is well drained; a sunny sandy bank would be ideal. Not suitable for shallow alkaline soils, while highly fertile sites produce very leggy plants.

HARDINESS: Moderately hardy to hardy.

SPECIAL CARE: No pruning required. To propagate the species sow seed in mid-spring. Take semi-ripe cuttings of 'Flore Pleno' in late summer.

SIZE: 1m x 85cm (3 x 2¾ft) after five years, ultimately 2m (6½ft) or more.

SIGNIFICANT PROBLEMS
None.

Recommended Varieties
Apart from the normal species, you will find 'Flore Pleno' (syn. 'Plenus') AGM, double yellow flowers, more compact and slower-growing, 75 x 60cm (2½ x 2ft) after five years, ultimately 1m (3ft).

Ulex europaeus 'Flore Pleno'

Vaccinium

FLOWERING or FRUITING INTEREST: Small flowers, usually pink or white in spring or summer. Black or red fruits.

FOLIAGE INTEREST: Small thick glossy leaves.

SUITABILITY AS HEDGING: None.

SITE AND SOIL: Full sun or moderate shade. Tolerates most moist soils, especially suitable for acidic, peaty or shady sites. Less hardy forms need shelter from cold winds. Low-growing types are excellent ground cover.

HARDINESS: Fairly hardy (*V. nummularia*) to moderately hardy (*V. vitis-idaea*).

SPECIAL CARE: Use conifer needles or other active material if possible when mulching. No pruning necessary other than to trim back the tips of vigorous shoots in spring. To propagate, take softwood cuttings with a heel in late summer, or plants can be layered.. Species can be raised from seed or plants can be layered.

SIZE: 15-20 x 20cm (5-8 x 8in) after five years, ultimately 30-40cm (1-1½ft) tall.

SIGNIFICANT PROBLEMS

Rabbits, deer.

Recommended Varieties

V. nummularia, thick glossy leaves, bronze when young then dark green, hairy shoots, pink flowers in late spring to early summer, black fruits, hardy only in mild areas but can be grown in alpine house. *V. vitis-idaea*, small dark green leaves with red tinge, white tinged pink summer flowers, bright red fruits, excellent ground cover for shade.

Vaccinium nummularia

Viburnum

" Not many shrub genera are as large as Viburnum, *as widely planted as* Viburnum, *as diverse as* Viburnum; *and yet really so little appreciated for their garden merits. There are over 150 species and, while some have undeniably lovely flowers or fruits, it is as foliage plants that most are grown in gardens. There isn't a shrubbery that shouldn't contain at least one of the evergreen species (and to be honest, not many that don't) and for anyone think of planting a screen of laurel, I suggest that before doing so, they look rather closely at the alternative choice of* V. tinus *'Lucidum' for a fine, dense and pretty fast growing screen. And having done so, look at a* Viburnum *before you make your choice of other shrubs too. "*

Viburnum x burkwoodii

FLOWERING or FRUITING INTEREST: Small white or pink flowers in spherical inflorescences in spring or summer; some are winter flowering, some are scented. Red, black or blue fruits that last into the winter.

FOLIAGE INTEREST: Fairly large dark green leaves, shape varies with species.

SUITABILITY AS HEDGING: *V. tinus* can be grown as an informal hedge.

SITE AND SOIL: Full sun to light shade, some tolerate deep shade. Most garden soils are suitable, including alkaline sites, but a few species are less successful on very wet or very dry soils. Large-leaved types need shelter from cold wind.

HARDINESS: Varies with species but most are moderately hardy to very hardy.

SPECIAL CARE: No pruning necessary but may be cut back in early spring to reduce size. To propagate, take semi-ripe cuttings in early summer or hardwood cuttings in winter.

SIZE: Most 1 x 1m (3 x 3ft) after five years, 3-4 x 3-4m (10-13 x 10-13ft) ultimately but varies with species.

SIGNIFICANT PROBLEMS
None.

Viburnum tinus 'Lucidum'

Recommended Varieties
V. x burkwoodii, semi-evergreen, rich green leaves with pale brown undersides, pink buds, scented white flowers in spring, intolerant of shade and extremely wet or dry soils, 2 x 1.2m (6 ½x 4ft) after five years. *V. davidii* AGM, large, oval leathery, dark green leaves, small white flowers in early summer, turquoise-blue fruits on female plants (if male present), intolerant of extremely wet or dry soils but tolerates wind and shade, 1 x 1m (3 x 3ft) after five years. *V. rhytidophyllum*, large dark green leaves with furrowed surface and grey woolly undersides, leaves droop in cold weather, small cream flowers in spring, red then black fruits, 1.5 x 1.2m (5 x 4ft) after five years. *V. tinus*, glossy dark green leaves, pink to white winter flowers, beautifully fragrant when outdoors but can be rather unpleasant when cut for the house, deep blue fruits ripening to black, intolerant of extremely wet or dry soils but good in shade, 1.2 x 1m (4 x 3ft); 'Eve Price' AGM, pink flowers from late winter, 1 x 1m (3 x 3ft) after five years; 'Gwenllian', pink flowers from late autumn; 'Lucidum', vigorous form with leaves and flowers larger than the species; 'Purpureum', very dark green leaves tinged with purple when young; 'Variegatum', dark green and cream leaves with silver undersides, small pink buds open to small white flowers from late autumn, black fruits, needs sun and shelter.

Vinca Periwinkle

FLOWERING or FRUITING INTEREST: Small tubular, usually blue flowers in early summer and intermittently until the autumn.

FOLIAGE INTEREST: Small to medium oval-shaped leaves, often variegated.

SUITABILITY AS HEDGING: None.

SITE AND SOIL: Full sun to deep shade in almost any garden soil except very dry sites. Vigorous trailing plants best used as leafy ground cover where little else will grow. To flower at all profusely, they require sun.

HARDINESS: Very hardy.

SPECIAL CARE: Plants require mulching in the first year after planting. No pruning necessary but a neat habit and fresh new growth will be encouraged by cutting back hard in spring with shears or a powered trimmer. To propagate, remove the naturally rooted layers or take semi-ripe cuttings in early summer or hardwood cuttings in winter.

SIZE: 1m x 60cm (3 x 2ft) after five years for V. major and 20 x 80cm (8in x 2½ft) for V. minor.

SIGNIFICANT PROBLEMS
Rust on V. major.

Recommended Varieties
V. major, medium-sized oval green leaves, bright blue flowers; 'Maculata' (syn. 'Aureomaculata'), dark yellow-green leaves with lighter margins, pale blue flowers; 'Variegata' AGM, light green leaves with pale yellow margins, blue-mauve flowers.
V. minor, small oval leaves, plain green, blue-pink or purple flowers; f. *alba*, white flowers; 'Argenteovariegata' AGM, dull green leaves with pale yellow margins and midribs, violet-blue flowers; 'Atro-purpurea' AGM, green leaves striped and edged with yellow, blue flowers; 'Azurea Flore Pleno' AGM, dark green leaves, red-purple flowers.

Vinca minor alba

Vinca major 'Variegata'

Vinca minor 'Argenteovariegata'

Vinca minor 'Azurea Flore Pleno'

CONIFERS

Abies Silver fir

❝*Silver firs are big plants and most gardens simply can't (or shouldn't) accommodate full-sized specimens of most species. But I couldn't ignore them because of a very common situation in conifers: among them are some dwarf or very slow growing and beautiful forms. Indeed, if you find there is one frustration above all in growing small conifers in small gardens, in that you will never see any cones, the slow-growing (although not dwarf) Korean fir will be your salvation.* ❞

FLOWERING or FRUITING INTEREST: Upright cones in spring after about 20 years although commonly after only five years on A. koreana – probably the youngest age at which any conifer cones are reliably formed.

FOLIAGE INTEREST: Glossy green flat needles usually have two grey-green or white stripes on the lower surfaces.

SUITABILITY AS HEDGING: None.

SITE AND SOIL: Avoid frost pockets that receive the early morning sun. Best in an acidic moist garden soil, not suitable for alkaline sites. Grows best in damp climates, intolerant of pollution.

HARDINESS: Hardy but needs protection from late spring frosts.

SPECIAL CARE: No pruning necessary. Sow seed for species, graft named varieties although this is difficult without special facilities.

SIZE: Varies with species.

SIGNIFICANT PROBLEMS

Adelgids.

Abies koreana 'Silberlocke'

Recommended Varieties

A. balsamea f. hudsonia AGM, dark green, aromatic, no cones, white resin-covered buds, a rounded dense bush, 30 x 30cm (1 x 1ft) after about five years, ultimately 80cm x 1m (2½ x 3ft). A. koreana, a very lovely plant, dark green needles, silver beneath, produces cones at a very young age, pyramidal, 1.5 x 1m (5 x 3ft) after five years then slowly to 10m (33ft); 'Silberlocke', twisted needles that reveal their silver undersides, half the size of the species. A. nordmanniana, has become popular as a Christmas tree, supposedly less prone to needle drop than more traditional Norway spruce, tolerates light shade, 8m (25ft) after 10 years. A. procera, blue-grey foliage, intolerant of dry or alkaline soils but good in exposed or partially shaded sites, 8m (25ft) after 10 years.

Araucaria araucana
Monkey puzzle

FLOWERING or FRUITING INTEREST: Cones sometimes form on upper branches. Most monkey puzzle trees are either male or female but there is no way of distinguishing the sexes until they flower.

FOLIAGE INTEREST: Stiff scale-like foliage in spirals around tiered branches.

SUITABILITY AS HEDGING: None.

SITE AND SOIL: Sun or light shade. Any welldrained soil and can tolerate fairly exposed sites.

HARDINESS: Hardy to very hardy.

SPECIAL CARE: The lower 2m (6½ ft) of the trunk of a young tree should be cleared of branches, otherwise no pruning required. To propagate, sow ripe seed in a cold frame.

SIZE: 6 x 3m (20 x 10ft) after 15 years, ultimately 20m (60ft) or more.

SIGNIFICANT PROBLEMS

None, although old trees tend to shed the lower branches.

> **Recommended Varieties**
> The normal species is widely grown.

Calocedrus decurrens
AGM   Incense cedar

FLOWERING or FRUITING INTEREST: Tiny male 'flowers' in winter. Insignificant female 'flowers'. Yellow-brown mature cones.

FOLIAGE INTEREST: Bright green scale-like upwardly growing foliage, very aromatic when crushed.

SUITABILITY AS HEDGING: Can make a slow-growing hedge for large gardens.

SITE AND SOIL: Sun or partial shade, shelter from cold drying winds. An acidic, fertile soil is preferred, on dry shallow soils the crown begins to thin. Useful on soils where honey fungus is a problem as it has considerable resistance.

HARDINESS: Hardy.

SPECIAL CARE: Keep the bottom 2 m (6 ft) of the trunk clear of shoots so the rich purple-brown trunk can be seen but otherwise no pruning is desirable. To propagate, sow seed in autumn or take hardwood cuttings in early autumn.

SIZE: 10 x 2m (33 x 6½ft) after 20 years, ultimately 40m (130ft) after 60 years.

SIGNIFICANT PROBLEMS

Scale insects.

> **Recommended Varieties**
> C. decurrens is the only species hardy in Britain.

Calocedrus decurrens

Araucaria araucana

Cedrus True cedars

> *It's commonly thought that most gardens contain cedar; even those without any trees. The reason is that the best garden greenhouses, sheds and other wooden structures are said to be of cedar rather than deal construction. In reality, the whole business is misleading; deal is most probably spruce (*Picea*) or pine (*Pinus*) and cedar is certainly not* Cedrus *but* Thuja. *Don't make the same mistake when choosing a tree; and don't make the mistake of choosing a full-sized* Cedrus *if your garden is small.*

FLOWERING or FRUITING INTEREST: Male 'flowers' resemble catkins. Female cones on trees at least 25 years old.

FOLIAGE INTEREST: Thin needle-like foliage in various shades of green and blue-green. A characteristic feature is the spiral of leaves on the short side-shoots and but single leaves on the long leading shoots.

SUITABILITY AS HEDGING: None.

SITE AND SOIL: Sun or partial shade, they thrive best in an acidic, moist fertile soil but will grow on dry alkaline soils.

HARDINESS: Hardy, but late spring frost can damage new growth.

SPECIAL CARE: Most cedars should not be pruned except the prostrate *C. libani* ssp. *libani* which can be trimmed. Cedar species come true from seed but named varieties must be grafted.

SIZE: Varies with species but approximately 5 x 2m (16 x 6½ft) after 10 years, ultimately 25m (80ft).

SIGNIFICANT PROBLEMS

Honey fungus, root rots, gale damage as the wood is rather brittle.

Cedrus libani atlantica 'Glauca Pendula'

Recommended Varieties

C. deodara AGM, blue-grey foliage when young ages to dark green, shoots droop attractively at the tips, conical shape, attractive when young, fast growing to 30m (100ft) but named varieties much smaller. *C. libani* ssp. *atlantica* (syn. *C. atlantica*), 3 x 2m (10 x 6½ft) after 10 years, ultimately over 25 x 25m (80 x 80ft); Glauca Group AGM, blue-silver foliage, one of the best blue conifers; 'Glauca Pendula', blue-green foliage, weeping branches that reach the ground, often need support, only 2 x 3m (6 x 10ft) after 10 years, ultimately 4 x 6m (13 x 20ft); *C. libani* ssp. *libani* AGM, very slow growing in either prostrate or densely conical form to about 1 x 2m (3 x 6½ft).

Chamaecyparis False cypress

FLOWERING or FRUITING INTEREST: None.

FOLIAGE INTEREST: Scale-like leaves form flat sprays and here is a wide range of colours: green, blue, silver and yellow.

SUITABILITY AS HEDGING: Excellent but choose varieties carefully as some are very fast growing and some have too open a habit.

SITE AND SOIL: Will tolerate light shade, but blue or yellow forms best in sun. Best in an acidic, clay soil but thrives on most fertile garden soils and is moderately lime tolerant.

HARDINESS: Hardy but can be damaged by heavy snow falls.

SPECIAL CARE: No pruning needed on specimen plants except to remove diseased or damaged branches in spring or autumn. To propagate, take heeled softwood cuttings or hardwood cuttings in spring or autumn. Clip hedges twice each year, in early summer and early autumn.

SIZE: Varies greatly with the species and variety.

SIGNIFICANT PROBLEMS

Aphids, adelgids, honey fungus, root rots, butt rot, *Phytophthora*.

Recommended Varieties

C. lawsoniana (Lawson cypress) is too large and gloomy for most gardens but the following varieties are suitable (note that this is a very small selection; there are more varieties of this plant than of any other tree); 'Chilworth Silver' AGM, blue-grey foliage, slow-growing dwarf, 3 x 1.5m (10 x 5ft); 'Columnaris', pale blue-grey foliage, grows 1m (3ft) every three years so position carefully, a slender column; 'Ellwoodii' AGM, grey-green foliage that turns blue in winter, narrow multi-stemmed tree 10m (33ft); 'Ellwood's Gold' AGM, yellow-green foliage, compact but narrow habit, 5m (16ft); 'Minima Aurea' AGM, golden yellow, compact egg-shaped dwarf, 80cm (2½ft); 'Minima Glauca' AGM, sea-green foliage, dwarf globe, 2 m (6½ft); 'Penbury Blue' AGM, bright silver-blue foliage, narrow habit, needs a warm site, 4 x 1.2m (13 x 4ft) in 10 years, ultimately twice this size; 'Pygmaea Argentea' AGM, dark blue-green foliage tipped with silver-white, can be scorched by direct sun, dwarf round bush, 30 x 30cm (1 x 1ft). *C. nootkatensis* 'Pendula' AGM, an extraordinary, narrow conical tree when young, and with foliage that hangs in 'curtains', often with blue cones, best shape when young, 6m (20ft) after 10 years, ultimately 20m (60ft). *C. obtusa* 'Crippsii' (syn. 'Crippsii Aurea') AGM, bright golden yellow ageing to green, 10 x 3m (33 x 10ft); 'Nana Gracilis' AGM, dark glossy green foliage, conical habit, 2m (6½ft). *C. pisifera* 'Boulevard' AGM, steel blue with white stripes on undersides, a good tree when young but rather a disappointing mess when older as the centre opens up and dies off, 6 x 3m (20 x 10ft); 'Filifera Aurea' AGM, golden yellow foliage, scorches in sun, spreading habit, 2.5 x 4.5m (8 x 14¾ft). *C. thyoides* 'Ericoides' AGM, sea-green foliage that turns purple-brown in winter, conical, 1.5m x 80cm (5 x 2½ft).

Chamaecyparis lawsoniana
'Penbury Blue'

CONIFERS

Cryptomeria japonica AGM Japanese Cedar

❝ *Although exquisitely shaped pine trees feature greatly in Japanese art and as subjects for Bonsai, any visitor to that country will soon discover that the great coniferous tree of Japan isn't* Pinus *but* Cryptomeria. *Vast forests of it clothe the central mountains, trains and lorries laden with its timber will be seen everywhere and countless buildings are built from it. It isn't however nearly as common as might be expected in European gardens; and that despite it having the unusual attribute among non-deciduous conifers of changing colour to a rich red in the autumn. Judging by my own experience, the reason may well be that its doesn't transplant well and if you persuade any other than a small specimen to establish, you will be fortunate.* ❞

FLOWERING or FRUITING INTEREST: Mature trees have small brown cones, green female flowers in spring, male flowers hidden.

FOLIAGE INTEREST: Needle-like foliage bright green or grey-green, often a bright red-bronze in winter. Red-brown bark, peels attractively in mature plants.

SUITABILITY AS HEDGING: None.

SITE AND SOIL: Tolerant of most garden soils although generally best on a moist, acidic site. May need shelter when young.

HARDINESS: Hardy.

SPECIAL CARE: No pruning needed. To propagate, take cuttings of named varieties in spring, the species can be raised from seed. Weeping branches of some forms layer rather easily and unusually for a conifer.

SIZE: 10 x 2.5m (30 x 8ft) after 20 years, 30m (100ft) ultimately.

SIGNIFICANT PROBLEMS
Honey fungus, *Phytophthora*.

> **Recommended Varieties**
> *C. japonica* AGM, broad columnar tree with sweeping branches, many smaller named varieties; 'Elegans', blue-green foliage in summer turns vivid bronze-red in winter and pale silver-green in spring, rounded tree, grows to 10m (30ft).

Cryptomeria japonica 'Elegans'

x *Cupressocyparis leylandii* Leyland cypress

FLOWERING or FRUITING INTEREST: Very small 'flowers' in spring and sometimes small round cones.

FOLIAGE INTEREST: Scale-like leaves in flat drooping sprays, dark green above, pale green below.

SUITABILITY AS HEDGING: Often used as hedging but very fast-growing and must not be planted in small gardens or where it will cause problems for neighbouring gardens. Very valuable in exposed sites to provide shelter.

SITE AND SOIL: Best in acidic or neutral soils but must be positioned carefully as it will starve any surrounding plants of light, moisture and nutrients.

HARDINESS: Hardy to very hardy.

SPECIAL CARE: Hedges should be clipped three or four times each year during the growing season.

SIZE: In the early stages, will grow 2m (6½ft), each year but the ultimate height is unknown because it is a relatively recent hybrid; there are already trees at least 35m (115ft) tall. None of the named varieties is significantly slower.

SIGNIFICANT PROBLEMS
Honey fungus.

> **Recommended Varieties**
> *C. l.* 'Castlewellan' (syn. 'Castlewellan Gold', 'Galway Gold'), golden yellow ageing to pale green with bronze tips, at least 15 x 3m (50 x 10ft); 'Robinson's Gold' AGM, is similar with old gold foliage.

x Cupressocyparis leylandii **'Castlewellan'**

Cupressus Cypress

FLOWERING or FRUITING INTEREST: Small yellow 'flowers' from late winter to early spring. Small rounded mature cones that turn from green to brown.

FOLIAGE INTEREST: Plumes of foliage give feathered outlines. Tiny scale-like foliage is aromatic and coloured green, blue or gold.

SUITABILITY AS HEDGING: Moderate; they tend to become rather open and gaunt with age unless clipped very frequently.

SITE AND SOIL: Sunny sheltered position away from cold winds. Any well drained soil is suitable. Very tolerant of hot, dry sites such as exposed sandy soils. Some make good coastal plantings.

Cupressus macrocarpa **'Goldcrest'**

HARDINESS: Hardy, although *C. macrocarpa* may be damaged in very cold winters.

SPECIAL CARE: Young trees may need protection from cold winter winds. No pruning needed except to remove diseased or damaged branches. To propagate, take cuttings in spring to summer. Clip hedges twice each year in early summer and early autumn.

SIZE: Varies with species.

SIGNIFICANT PROBLEMS
Phytophthora, aphids, canker.

Recommended Varieties
C. macrocarpa 'Goldcrest' AGM, bright golden yellow foliage, the best yellow form although prone to aphid damage, a narrow conical tree, up to 15m (50ft); 'Golden Pillar', golden yellow foliage, a small tree with narrow habit. *C. sempervirens* 'Stricta' (syn. 'Pyramidalis') AGM, fastigiate habit, fast growing when young but then slower, rarely more than 15m (50ft).

Juniperus Juniper

"*Although I have said that conifers (at least in the form of their natural species) are trees, not shrubs, the juniper probably comes closest to confounding this assertion, at least among common forms. It's one of only three native British conifers (yew and Scots pine are the others) and if you see it growing wild, it usually takes the form of a spreading or more or less rounded shrub, very rarely a tree. In truth, in its wild form, it is often a ragged, straggly thing, but few species take on such a transformation when their cultivated variants are compared with the native plant. For some of them are so tightly growing and compact as to seem almost solid. And when two or three exotic species, especially the Oriental* Juniperus chinensis *and the North American* J. horizontalis *are included too, the result is a remarkable array of quite invaluable dwarf conifers for gardens and commercial plantings almost everywhere.* "

FLOWERING or FRUITING INTEREST: Tiny 'flowers' at shoot tips. Small blue or black mature cones only if both male and female plants are present.

FOLIAGE INTEREST: Young foliage is sharp and needle-like but ages to become fleshy scales. Foliage may be green, yellow, grey or blue.

SUITABILITY AS HEDGING: None.

SITE AND SOIL: Full sun to light shade with shelter from cold winds.

Juniperus communis **'Compressa'**

Tolerates most garden soils even when dry and alkaline.

HARDINESS: Hardy to very hardy.

SPECIAL CARE: No pruning needed, although can be trimmed back lightly but will not regenerate from very old wood. To propagate, take semi-ripe cuttings in summer or hardwood cuttings in winter although rooting is often difficult without misting.

SIZE: Varies greatly with species.

SIGNIFICANT PROBLEMS

Aphids, *Phytophthora*, red spider mite.

Juniperus horizontalis 'Blue Chip'

Juniperus sabina 'Tamariscifolia'

Recommended Varieties

J. chinensis 'Expansa Variegata' (syn. *J. davurica* 'Expansa Variegata'), sage-green foliage with cream-white sprays, forms a low mound, ultimately 1 x 3m (3 x 10ft). *J. communis* 'Compressa' AGM, grey foliage ageing to green, shelter from cold or salt winds, for rock gardens or containers. A remarkable plant that when well grown looks more like a chess piece than a shrub.very slow growing, ultimate height 1m x 30cm (3 x 2ft); 'Hibernica' AGM, silver-blue foliage, needs acidic soil, forms a narrow column, very slow-grow-

ing, 6m x 60 cm (20 x 2ft) after 100 years; 'Repanda' AGM, grey-green foliage with bronze tinge in winter, dwarf creeping habit, good ground cover for a sunny site, 30cm x 2m (1 x 6½ft) after 10 years. *J. horizontalis* 'Blue Chip' (syn. 'Blue Moon'), distinctive blue foliage, retains the same colour all year round, carpeting habit, 50cm x 3m (20 in x 10ft). *J. x pfitzeriana* (syn. x *media*) 'Old Gold' AGM, bronze-gold foliage, does not fade in winter, slow-growing, 1 x 2m (3 x 61/2ft). *J. sabina* 'Tamariscifolia', dark green foliage with unpleasant smell when crush-

ed, shoot tips tend to die back after hard frosts, very attractive when grown between rocks, at edge of raised beds or on sandy banks, 20 x 30cm (8in x 1ft) after 10 years, ultimately 1 x 1.2m (3 x 4ft). *J. squamata* 'Blue Carpet' AGM, blue-grey foliage, sharp needles, slow growing, 30cm x 1.2m (1 x 4ft); 'Blue Star' AGM, silver-blue foliage, 60cm x 1m (2 x 3ft) after 30 years. *J. virginiana* 'Sulphur Spray' (syn. *J. chinensis* 'Sulphur Spray') AGM, pale sulphur yellow foliage, sometimes mottled, 2 x 2m (6½ x 6½ ft) after 30 years.

Picea Spruce

❝*It's ironic that the best known, most loved species of spruce and the one species that I can guarantee everyone has seen and knows on sight is probably the worst of all for growing in gardens. The Norway spruce,* Picea abies, *is the almost universal choice as a Christmas tree in Britain (although some inroads have been made in replacing it with such plants as* Abies nordmanniana *in recent years). Decorated and lit up for the festive season,* P. abies *is a fine thing. But in the garden, it is of open habit, straggly, prone to turn brown, drop its needles and be thoroughly unappealing. And by another irony, much the most widely planted spruce tree in Britain, the Sitka spruce,* P. sitchensis, *while a mainstay of British forestry, is equally useless in gardens. So having dismissed two species, I urge you strongly to explore some of the remainder in the genus; and be very agreeably surprised.* ❞

FLOWERING or FRUITING INTEREST: Insignificant 'flowers' in late winter to spring. Green cones age to brown although the many named dwarf varieties do not usually produce cones.
FOLIAGE INTEREST: Long single needles, superficially like firs but the needles are borne on short woody pegs that remain after the leaves have fallen.
SUITABILITY AS HEDGING: None.
SITE AND SOIL: Open site, intolerant of shade. They will grow on most garden soils except very poor dry or very alkaline sites. Not good plants for coastal areas.
HARDINESS: Mainly hardy but late spring frost can damage young trees and the new growth.

SPECIAL CARE: No pruning necessary; spruces do not regenerate from old wood and pruning can spoil the shape. Any necessary removal of damaged branches should happen in winter. Difficult to propagate without a misting facility.

Picea glauca albertiana **'Conica'**

Picea omorika **'Nana'**

SIGNIFICANT PROBLEMS

Honey fungus, aphids, red spider mite, galls, adelgids, diebacks, various rots, and rusts.

Picea pungens **'Hoopsii'**

Recommended Varieties

P. abies 'Nidiformis' AGM, short light green needles, very slow-growing, compact, flat-topped bush, 50 x 80cm (1¾ x 2½ft) after 20 years. *P. breweriana* AGM, blue-green foliage with white stripes, red 'flowers' followed by long cones in late spring, a weeping tree, best in a sheltered site away from water-logged soil, ideal lawn specimen, tolerates alkalinity if the soil is moist, 4 x 2.4m (13 x 6¾ft) after 20 years. *P. glauca albertiana* 'Conica' AGM, green needles with new growth bright light green, very hardy,

slow-growing, conical tree, 1.5 x 1.5m (5 x 5ft) after 20 years. *P. mariana* 'Nana' AGM, blue-green foliage on yellow-brown shoots, rounded cushion shape, 60 x 40cm (2 x 1½ft). *P. omorika* AGM, glossy dark green foliage with blue-white undersides, red 'flowers' are fol-lowed by narrow mature cones, very hardy, tolerates pollution and poor or alkaline soils although prone to honey fungus, a columnar tree with pendulous branches that turn up at the tips, 7 x 2.4m (23 x 6¾ft) after 10 years, 15m (50ft) after 20; 'Nana', conspicuous bands on the

needles are an attractive feature, conical bush, 1.2 x 1.2m (4 x 4ft) after 15 years. *P. orientalis* 'Aurea' AGM, bright yellow late spring foliage ageing to pale green, crimson 'flowers' in spring, mature cones that ripen to brown, 6 x 3m (20 x 10ft) after 10 years, 15m (50 ft) after 20 years. *P. pungens* 'Hoopsii' AGM, striking blue-white foliage, narrow conical shape, 5 x 1.5m (16 x 5ft) after 20 years; 'Koster' AGM, (note that several forms are grown under this name), silver-blue foliage, slow-growing, narrow conical tree, 3 x 1m (10 x 3ft) after 20 years.

Pinus Pine

" *Pines are uniquely different from other garden conifers in their relatively long needles. They have a very different and stylish appearance, but in few other conifer genera is it as important to choose varieties carefully. Some are very large and many very straggly.* "

FLOWERING or FRUITING INTEREST: Male and female 'flowers' appear in separate clusters on new shoots usually in spring. Mature cones rather ragged in form.

FOLIAGE INTEREST: Relatively long needles, very long in some species. The

Pinus montezumae

groups within the genus are distinguished by the numbers of needles within each cluster: two, three or five.

SUITABILITY AS HEDGING: None.

SITE AND SOIL: Open, intolerant of shade. Some of the long-needled pines need shelter from cold winds and late frosts. An acidic soil in a dry site is ideal although some are tolerant of other soils.

HARDINESS: Those I recommend here are all hardy to very hardy in Britain.

SPECIAL CARE: No pruning is necessary and best avoided as the plants don't regenerate from old wood. Propagation is difficult without a misting facility.

SIZE: Varies greatly with species.

SIGNIFICANT PROBLEMS

Honey fungus, *Phytophthora*, rusts, adelgids, sawflies, pine shoot moth caterpillars.

Recommended Varieties

P. contorta, yellow-green foliage, two-needled, not for alkaline sites, ideal for light sandy or stony soils or coastal areas, vigorous, 6m (20ft) after 10 years, 20m (66ft) ultimately. *P. heldreichii* var. *leucodermis* 'Compact Gem', two-needled, ideal for rock gardens, very slow-growing, rounded bush, 1m x 40cm (3 x 1½ft) in 40 years. *P. montezumae*, very beautiful when mature, grey-green foliage, five-needled, long sharp needles on red-brown shoots, male 'flowers' red, female 'flowers' purple, long blue-purple cones, fairly hardy to moderately hardy, needs shelter, 6 x 1.5m (20 x 5ft) after 10 years, ultimately 20 x 20m (66 x 66ft).

P. mugo 'Mops' AGM, bright green foliage, two-needled, attractive brown buds in winter, an irregularly rounded bush, 75 x 75 cm (30 x 30 in); *P. m.* var. *pumilio* AGM, dark foliage, white winter buds, small purple cones that ripen to dark brown, creeping habit, 2 x 3 m (6 x 10 ft) ultimately. *P. nigra* AGM, dense dark foliage, two-needled, useful as a shelter belt on alkaline sites, tolerates most soils and pollution, 5m (16ft) after 10 years, 30m (100ft) ultimately. *P. parviflora* 'Adcock's Dwarf' AGM, grey-green foliage, five-needled, slow-growing compact bush, 2.5 x 1.2m (8 x 4ft) in 30 years. *P. radiata* AGM, bright green foliage, three-needled, tolerates shallow

alkaline soils but then shorter lived (about 30 years), useful shelter in mild coastal areas, 10m (33ft) in 10 years, 40m (130ft) ultimately. *P. strobus* 'Radiata' (syn. 'Nana') AGM, blue-green foliage, five-needled yellow male 'flowers', pink female 'flowers', green banana-like cones that ripen to brown, irregularly rounded and spreading, 1.2 x 1.2m (4 x 4ft) ultimately. *P. sylvestris* AGM, the only British native pine, blue-grey foliage, two-needled, pink coloured bark on mature trees (a ready way to distinguish it at a distance from *P. nigra*), yellow male 'flowers', pink female 'flowers', egg-shaped cones are green then brown, fast growing when young,

Pinus wallichiana

6 x 2m (20 x 6½ft) after 10 years, then ultimately 35 x 4m (115 x 13ft); 'Aurea' AGM, golden yellow colour best in winter, slow growing and bushy; 'Fastigiata', suits any soil, tall but narrow, ultimately 15 x 2m (50 x 6½ft); 'Watereri (syn. 'Nana'), blue-grey foliage, very stiff needles, rather effective among heathers, dwarf upright conical tree, 4 x 4m (13 x 13ft) ultimately. *P. wallichiana* (syn. *P. griffithii*) AGM, graceful, five-needled, needs sun, any soil except thin and alkaline, fast-growing for first 20 years, bright green resinous cones after 10 years, 8m (25ft) after 10 years, ultimately 30m (100 ft).

Pseudotsuga menziesii AGM Douglas fir

FLOWERING or FRUITING INTEREST: Slender conical buds. 'Flowers' inconspicuous. The cones are pendulous and fall intact.

FOLIAGE INTEREST: Dark green foliage with two white bands on the undersides. The leaves are soft textured and have a sweet, caramel aroma when crushed.

SUITABILITY AS HEDGING: None.

SITE AND SOIL: Sun or light shade. A sheltered damp site with plenty of space is essential. On dry and alkaline sites, the trees become thin and chlorotic.

HARDINESS: Hardy to very hardy although the early new growth can suffer from frost damage.

SPECIAL CARE: No routine pruning but young plants commonly develop two leading shoots; the weaker should be removed. Propagate by seed sown in spring outdoors or by grafting.

SIZE: 8m (25ft) after 10 years, 60m (195ft) ultimately; all of the tallest growing trees in Britain are of this species.

SIGNIFICANT PROBLEMS
None.

Recommended Varieties
P. menziesii is a tall forest tree grown for timber and only suitable for the very largest gardens, but there are smaller forms such as *P. m.* 'Glauca Pendula' AGM, a small weeping tree with silver-blue foliage which reaches 10m (33ft) ultimately.

Pseudotsuga menziesii **'Glauca Pendula'**

Taxus baccata AGM Yew

" Although not a typical conifer, the yew is probably the most beautiful, the most useful and the most misunderstood of them all. It can be clipped more closely and neatly than any other, it regenerates from old wood in a most untypical manner; but no, it isn't slow growing. Visitors to my own garden have frankly not believed the fact that I planted my yew hedging as recently as I did. Within 10 years, it has real height, real thickness and a look of genuine maturity. I must be honest and add that I purchased well grown plants, and they weren't cheap; but big yews do transplant with ease; and that's a great deal more than can be said for most other conifers. Yes, it's true that both botanically and in the way it behaves as a cultivated plant, yew is not typical of the group. "

FLOWERING or FRUITING INTEREST: Yew plants are either male or female; females produce scarlet 'fruit'.

FOLIAGE INTEREST: Dark green, dense foliage comprising flattened needles. Coloured and variegated forms are also available.

SUITABILITY AS HEDGING: The finest of all hedge plants, dense, long-lived and regenerating from very old wood.

SITE AND SOIL: Full sun to moderate shade, can be stunted by severe wind. Any soils, even on highly alkaline sites, are suitable. Yellow-foliaged types can scorch in full sun.

HARDINESS: Very hardy.

SPECIAL CARE: No pruning is needed for free-standing trees or dwarf specimens although old or overgrown plants can be cut back hard and will regenerate from old wood. Hedges and topiary plants should be clipped once or preferably twice in early summer and early autumn. To propagate, stratify ripe seed or take hardwood cuttings in winter. Almost all parts are highly poisonous.

SIZE: 2 x 1.2m (6 x 4ft) after 10 years, 4 x 2.5m (13 x 8ft) after 20 years, but yew is the longest lived tree in Britain and trees of many hundreds of years of age can be 30 x 20m (100 x 60ft).

SIGNIFICANT PROBLEMS
None.

Taxus baccata 'Standishii'

Recommended Varieties
There are many forms of *T. baccata* that differ markedly from the parent; 'Fastigiata' (syn. 'Hibernica') AGM, Irish yew, female, a common churchyard yew, very dark green needles, almost vertical branches, 1.5m x 50cm (5 x 1¾ft) in five years; 'Repandens' AGM, female, very dark green foliage, spreading, semi-prostrate, 30-60cm x 1m (1-2½ x 3ft) after five years; 'Standishii' AGM, female, golden foliage, needs full sun, upright columnar, 1.5 x 30cm (5 x 1ft) in 10 years; 'Summergold', male, new growth is yellow later turning to green with yellow border, prefers sun, ideal ground cover, 50cm x 1.5m (1¾ x 5ft).

Thuja False cedar, Arbor vitae

FLOWERING or FRUITING INTEREST: Tiny insignificant greenish cones become brown at maturity.

FOLIAGE INTEREST: Small, cypress-like needles, with a pleasant aroma, typically narrowly pyramidal in shape.

SUITABILITY AS HEDGING: Very good, and could be planted more much frequently instead of cypresses.

SITE AND SOIL: Full sun to light shade. *Thuja* is more tolerant of wind exposure than cypresses although it will still be browned by salt spray. Best on deep moist soil.

HARDINESS: Very hardy.

SPECIAL CARE: Hedges should be clipped once or twice during the growing

Recommended Varieties

T. occidentalis 'Danica' AGM, bright green turning more golden in winter, neat rounded habit, ideal for rock gardens, 50 x 50 cm (20 x 20 in) after 20 years; 'Holmstrup' AGM, glossy rich green, pointed spire shape, 2.5 m x 50 cm (8 ft x 20 in) after 20 years; 'Rheingold' AGM, deep gold with amber tints, slow-growing conical bush, 2 x 1.5 m (6 x 5 ft) after 20 years.

T. orientalis (syn. *Platycladus orientalis*) 'Aurea Nana' AGM, soft yellow-green, globe-shaped, 75 x 45 cm (30 x 18 in) ultimately; 'Rosedalis', bright yellow in spring, sea-green in summer then plum-purple in winter, dense and slow-growing, egg-shaped, 80 x 40 cm (32 x 16 in) after 20 years.

T. plicata, bright green with white markings on undersides, a fresh pineapple or fruit drop aroma, 10 x 2 m (30 x 6 ft) after 20 years but usually grown as a hedge; 'Rogersii', dark golden yellow and bronze foliage, neat rounded habit, 45 x 45 cm (18 x 18 in); 'Stoneham Gold' AGM, green with copper-gold new growth, ideal for rock gardens or containers, narrow conical tree, 3 x 1 m (10 x 3 ft) after 20 years; 'Zebrina', striking green and gold stripes, grow in direct sun for the best stripes.

Thuja plicata

season, the foliage causes a skin rash on many people (unpleasant, as I know from personal experience) so wear gloves when clipping. Damaged trees will regenerate fairly well from old wood. To propagate, stratify ripe seed or take hardwood cuttings in winter.
SIZE: Varies greatly with species.

SIGNIFICANT PROBLEMS

Honey fungus, rots.

Tsuga Hemlock

FLOWERING or FRUITING INTEREST: Male and female 'flowers' on the same tree; small mature cones.
FOLIAGE INTEREST: Small, soft cypress-like needles, typically narrowly pyramidal. Dark green or blue-green upper surface and white undersides.

SUITABILITY AS HEDGING: Makes a superb and highly under-appreciated dense hedge.
SITE AND SOIL: Full sun to moderate shade, a good choice for windy sites. Most garden soils are suitable but the ideal site is slightly acidic and free-draining.
HARDINESS: Hardy
SPECIAL CARE: No pruning is needed unless grown as a hedge when it should be clipped once or twice during the growing season. Propagate by stratifying ripe seed.
SIZE: 4 x 1.5m (13 x 5ft) after five years or 40m (130ft) ultimately.

SIGNIFICANT PROBLEMS

Honey fungus.

Recommended Varieties

T. canadensis 'Jeddeloh' AGM, bright green foliage, tolerates alkalinity, neat low mound, 45 x 60cm (1½ x 2ft). *T. heterophylla* AGM, dark green foliage with silver-white undersides, bright red 'flowers', cones green with purple tinges, tolerates water-logging, a large tree, 18 x 7m (56 x 23ft) after 20 years.

Tsuga heterophylla

NON-CONIFEROUS TREES

Arbutus Strawberry tree

❝ Gardeners too often become excited at the thought of the strawberry tree. It isn't however what you might think because its fruit only looks like strawberries. But consider it not as what it isn't, but as what it is and your garden will be the richer for a lovely evergreen tree that offers appeal and interest in almost all of its features. ❞

FLOWERING or FRUITING INTEREST: Small white flowers in late autumn; at the same time red, yellow or orange (edible but not very pleasant) fruits from the previous year are still present on the tree.

FOLIAGE INTEREST: Dark glossy green foliage. Some species also have attractive red or brown peeling bark.

SUITABILITY AS HEDGING: None.

SITE AND SOIL: A position in full sun is best but they can tolerate light shade. Shelter from cold winds is essential when the trees are young. Most soils are suitable including alkaline and dry sites but avoid water-logged positions. Can withstand exposure in mild coastal areas.

HARDINESS: Moderately hardy when established.

SPECIAL CARE: No pruning is necessary but they will regenerate fairly well if it is necessary to cut back into old wood. To propagate, sow seed in spring. *A. unedo* can be raised from semi-ripe cuttings taken in midsummer.

SIZE: 3-5m (10-16ft) after 10 years.

SIGNIFICANT PROBLEMS
Leaf spots, aphids.

Arbutus x andrachnoides

Recommended Varieties
A. x andrachnoides AGM, a natural hybrid found growing wild in Greece, dull pale green foliage, rich red flaking bark, white flowers in late autumn and winter, fruiting not reliable, 5 x 3.5m (16 x 12ft) after 10 years, ultimately 9-10m (30-3 ft).

A. unedo AGM, the classic Killamey strawberry tree of Ireland, brown-grey bark, honey-scented white flowers, orange-red fruits, not completely reliable in cold areas, 3 x 3m (10 x 10ft) after 10 years, ultimately 10m (33ft); *A. u. rubra* AGM, pink flowers, abundant fruits.

Embothrium coccineum Chilean fire bush

FLOWERING or FRUITING INTEREST: Spidery red flowers in late spring or early summer.

FOLIAGE INTEREST: Leathery dark green foliage, sometimes partly deciduous.

SUITABILITY AS HEDGING: None.

SITE AND SOIL: Sunny sheltered site such as a suitable, warm wall. Requires an acidic or neutral soil that is moist but well drained; it will not tolerate alkalinity.

HARDINESS: Moderately hardy to hardy but damaged by late frosts.

SPECIAL CARE: No pruning is necessary but frost damaged branches should be removed after flowering. Propagate by seed, removal of suckers from the parent plant or by semi-ripe cuttings.

SIZE: 3 x 1m (10 x 3ft) after 10 years, ultimately 9m (30ft).

SIGNIFICANT PROBLEMS
None.

Recommended Varieties
The true species is normally grown in Britain although 'Norquinco' is more floriferous with orange-red flowers.

Embothrium coccineum

Eucalyptus Gum tree

FLOWERING or FRUITING INTEREST: White flowers with no petals but long stamens are produced in summer on trees more than about 10 years old. Striking, often globular fruits may follow.

FOLIAGE INTEREST: Young foliage is usually oval and silver-blue in colour, mature foliage is lance-shaped and grey-green. Bark peels off older trees revealing attractive cream and brown markings.

SUITABILITY AS HEDGING: Some make surprisingly good if rather lax hedges when pruned hard.

SITE AND SOIL: Full sun in a sheltered position. Soil should be moist but well-drained. Most are intolerant of alkalinity. Position carefully, not only because they are very conspicuous trees but also because their roots can damage walls.

HARDINESS: Most eucalypts are tender in Britain but those I recommend here are moderately hardy although always best when sheltered from cold winds.

SPECIAL CARE: A deep (15cm/6in) mulch overwinter will give valuable crown protection. Prune hard in early spring to encourage the attractive young foliage and a shrubby habit. Propagate by sowing seed in warmth in spring or early summer.

SIZE: Most will attain 15 x 6m (50 x 20ft) after 15-20 years, ultimately 20-30m (60-100ft) but by annual pruning they can be kept to any size; most grow about 1m (3ft) in a year. Be careful as they can easily become too big for your garden.

SIGNIFICANT PROBLEMS

Silver leaf disease, oedema, which causes warty patches on the foliage (improve drainage and prune to improve air circulation), aphids. *E. gunnii* is notoriously prone to rabbit damage

Eucalyptus pauciflora

Ilex Holly

❝*Largely thorough its pagan and then more recently Christian symbolism, the name holly has become associated in people's minds with a prickly, red-fruited evergreen tree that is noticed in winter but rather overlooked at other times of the year. In most respects, this gives a distorted impression; and indeed, a distorted impression not of the holly but of the large and generally unappreciated group of over 400 species that comprises the entire genus* Ilex. *Not all have red fruits, many aren't prickly and some aren't even evergreen, but many of those that are make excellent, and generally small, garden trees, a few indeed of little more than shrub size although I have included them in this part of the book for convenience.* ❞

FLOWERING or FRUITING INTEREST: Some female plants have very attractive red, black or yellow fruits if males are present nearby.

FOLIAGE INTEREST: Glossy green, dark green or blue-green foliage. Some have spines, many have attractive yellow or silver-white variegations.

SUITABILITY AS HEDGING: Most hollies make excellent, dense, although slow growing hedges.

SITE AND SOIL: Full sun to moderate shade. Tolerate most garden soils if not water-logged. Can withstand exposure, pollution and some salt spray.

HARDINESS: Hardy to very hardy.

SPECIAL CARE: Hollies respond well to being pruned to shape but take care not to cut back into old, hard wood as it does not regenerate satisfactorily, but clip lightly to shape plants. The leading shoot may be pruned to restrict the height. All-green shoots on variegated hollies should be cut out. Hedges may be lightly clipped twice a year in midsummer and in early autumn. Hollies are tricky to propagate although the species come true from seed stratified in the autumn. Layering is sometimes effective but striking cuttings is a chancy business.

SIZE: Varies with species, most are slow growing, attaining 1m x 50cm (3 x 1¾ft) after five years, ultimately some can form 15m (50ft) trees.

SIGNIFICANT PROBLEMS

Harmless leaf miner larvae disfigure foliage, birds feed on fruits.

Ilex x *altaclarensis* '**Golden King**'

Ilex x *altaclarensis* '**Lawsoniana**'

Ilex aquifolium 'Ferox'

Ilex x meservae 'Blue Angel'

Recommended Varieties

[All female forms have red fruits unless stated otherwise.]

I. x altaclarensis, large, glossy but not usually very spiny foliage, fast-growing so ideal for hedges, upright tree, 2.5 x 1m (8 x 3ft) after 10 years, 8m (25ft) ultimately; 'Golden King' AGM, female (despite the name), large leaves with gold margin, 'Lawsoniana' AGM, female, foliage is two shades of green with yellow centre, dull red fruits. *I. aquifolium* AGM, dark green foliage, wavy edge with spines, bright red fruits, good for hedging, small conical tree, 3 x 1.2m (10 x 4ft) after 10 years, 20m (60ft) ultimately; 'Argentea Marginata Pendula', female, foliage has broad silver-white margins, weeping shrub or tree of about 3m (10ft); 'Bacciflava' (syn. 'Fructu Luteo'), female, dark green foliage, lemon-yellow fruits, upright tree 9m (30ft) ultimately; 'Ferox', male, many spines on margin and on leaf surface; 'Ferox Argentea', male, silver-white edges to dark green foliage, purple shoots; 'Golden Queen' (syn. 'Aurea Regina') AGM, male (despite the name), dark foliage with gold edges, spiny; 'Golden Van Tol', female, dark green foliage with yellow margins, few spines, small shrub; 'Handsworth New Silver' AGM, female, dark foliage with clear white margin, spiny, dark purple shoots; 'J. C. van Tol' AGM, female, narrow foliage, few spines, self-pollinating; 'Pyramidalis', female, dark green foliage, self-pollinating, conical tree; 'Silver Queen' (syn. 'Argentea Regina') AGM, male, dark green foliage with white margin, young foliage pink, conical habit, 5m (16ft) ultimately. *I. crenata* 'Golden Gem' AGM, female, small pale green-yellow foliage with some variegation, needs sun in early part of the year, few fruits, low growing up to 2 x 2m (6½ x 6½ft). *I. x meservae* 'Blue Angel' AGM, female, one of a curious group of hybrids that have been developed in recent years in the United States. glossy blue-green foliage that turns purple-green in winter (not really blue as is often claimed), spiny but soft to touch, slow growing.

Eucryphia

❝ *Many plant species, and many plant varieties have names that are pretty self-explanatory. Others are almost invariably a puzzle and the best form of this quite lovely small tree is one of them. Let's start at the beginning. Eucryphia is straightforward if a little unusual: from the Greek meaning well covered, a reference to the sepals fusing at their tips to form a small cap over the petals. The hybrid name* x nymansensis *(meaning 'of Nymans') is also clear if you are familiar with the great house of Nymans in Sussex in whose nursery its parents* Eucryphia cordifolia *and* E. glutinosa *first hybridised around the time of the First World War. But 'Nymansay'? Among the seed-ling plants raise at Nymans, two were particularly good and someone wrote on their labels* Nymans A *and* Nymans B. Nymans A *was the better and it received an award from the Royal Horticultural Society in 1924 by which time it needed a proper name. Having been called* Nymans A *for several years, 'Nymansay' it officially became.* ❞

FLOWERING or FRUITING INTEREST: Superb white flowers with prominent stamens appear in late summer to autumn on trees over 10 years old.
FOLIAGE INTEREST: Dull green foliage.
SUITABILITY AS HEDGING: None.
SITE AND SOIL: Light to moderate shade at the base with flowers in full sun. Needs shelter from cold winds. Soil should be acidic with plenty of humus, deep and moist but not water-logged. Of the species listed here only *E. x nymansensis* tolerates alkalinity.
HARDINESS: Moderately hardy, given shelter from cold winter winds.
SPECIAL CARE: Mulch with acidic material such as conifer needles. Protect young plants in winter. Avoid pruning other than to remove damaged branches in spring. To propagate, take semi-ripe cuttings in early summer, or try layering which is effective with some species. Unlikely to come true from seed.
SIZE: 2 x 1m (6½ x 3ft) after five years then slowly attains 10 x 4m (33 x 13ft) in favourable sites.

SIGNIFICANT PROBLEMS
None.

Eucryphia x nymansensis **'Nymansay'**

Recommended Varieties
E. x intermedia 'Rostrevor' AGM, white flowers with yellow centres from late summer to early autumn, free flowering, fast growing. *E. milliganii*, dark green foliage with blue-green undersides, small white flowers in midsummer, flowers on 7-10 year old trees, slow-growing upright tree. *E. x nymansensis*, masses of white flowers in summer, tolerates alkalinity, the hardiest and most reliable for most gardens, a small columnar tree; 'Nymansay', very dark green sombre foliage, fragrant large white flowers, fast growing.

Magnolia grandiflora Southern magnolia, Bull bay

FLOWERING or FRUITING INTEREST: Huge white saucer-like flowers which are fragrant and produced over a long period from late summer to autumn. The varieties I recommend should begin flowering when plants are five to seven years old.

FOLIAGE INTEREST: Large to very large oval foliage, glossy and dark green with (more or less, depending on variety) brown felt-like indumentum on the undersides.

SUITABILITY AS HEDGING: None.

SITE AND SOIL: Full sun to moderate shade with shelter from cold winds, often grown against sunny walls but I have a free-standing tree in a fairly sheltered spot in my own, rather cold garden. Tolerates most garden soils but least reliable on dry and alkaline sites.

HARDINESS: Hardy, but best with shelter from cold winter winds and the rather brittle branches will be damaged by heavy snow falls.

SPECIAL CARE: No pruning necessary but branches broken overwinter should be cut back to the junction with the next major shoot. If growing against a wall, spur prune to within 30cm (1ft) of the framework in spring to maintain

Magnolia grandiflora 'Goliath'

a neat habit. To propagate selected forms, take semi-ripe cuttings in summer but these are more reliable if grafted on to the species rootstock. Seed-raised plants can take up to 30 years to flower.

SIZE: 3 x 2m (10 x 6½ft) after five years, 8 x 5m (25 x 16ft) ultimately in favourable sites.

SIGNIFICANT PROBLEMS
None.

Recommended Varieties
The normal species is as good as any for foliage appeal but best flowering will come from forms such as: 'Goliath', very large flowers on younger trees, hardier, wavy-edged foliage with less indumentum on undersides; 'Exmouth' AGM, flowers when young, hardy.

Nothofagus Southern beech

FLOWERING or FRUITING INTEREST: Insignificant flowers in spring.

FOLIAGE INTEREST: Small very dark green foliage that is blunt-toothed, borne on sticky red shoots.

SUITABILITY AS HEDGING: None.

SITE AND SOIL: Avoid frost, exposed sites, dry conditions and alkaline soils. Position where they can be given plenty of space, as a lawn specimen for example.

HARDINESS: Barely hardy to fairly hardy.

SPECIAL CARE: No pruning necessary. Propagate by sowing ripe seed during the autumn months.

SIZE: 15 x 6m (50 x 20ft).

SIGNIFICANT PROBLEMS
None.

Recommended Varieties
N. betuloides, oval glossy dark green foliage, broad columnar tree, 15 x 6m (50 x 20ft); not to be confused with the much more familiar deciduous *N. antarctica*.

Nothofagus betuloides

Quercus ilex AGM Holm oak

❝There can be no more familiar, more fondly loved and more splendid British tree than the oak. Sadly, it finds no place in this book because both native species are deciduous. But just as I have remarked that many people are surprised at the notion of deciduous hollies, so many people are amazed to discover that of the 600 species of oak, a very large number are evergreen. Most are too big, too tender or too unattractive for gardens but this one is tough and although on the gloomy side, it has the advantage of being probably the biggest evergreen tree hardy in Britain. For that reason, it is invaluable where large scale screening is needed in big gardens. ❞

FLOWERING or FRUITING INTEREST: Gold male catkins briefly in early summer. Small fertile green acorns after hot summers.

FOLIAGE INTEREST: Leathery rather dull dark green foliage with grey undersides. Dark-coloured bark.

SUITABILITY AS HEDGING: Useful as a windbreak in coastal gardens.

SITE AND SOIL: Open sunny position but can tolerate light shade. Any deep well-drained soil. Thrives best in mild areas particularly near the sea.

HARDINESS: Hardy but will be severely browned in cold winters.

SPECIAL CARE: No routine pruning and any necessary to remove damaged branches should be done in late winter. To propagate, sow ripe acorns in autumn.

SIZE: 6 x 5m (20 x 16ft) after 20 years, ultimately 25m (80ft) tall.

SIGNIFICANT PROBLEMS
None.

Recommended Varieties
The true species is the only form available.

Sophora microphylla

Sophora microphylla

FLOWERING or FRUITING INTEREST: Hanging clusters of pea-like yellow flowers in late spring on mature trees. Long seedpods. All parts of the plant are poisonous.

FOLIAGE INTEREST: Narrow pinnate dark green foliage.

SUITABILITY AS HEDGING: None.

SITE AND SOIL: Full sun in a sheltered site. Any fertile, well-drained soil.

HARDINESS: Barely hardy to fairly hardy.

SPECIAL CARE: If training against a wall, tie in shoots to horizontal wire supports. No pruning necessary. To propagate, sow seed in a greenhouse in spring or take semi-ripe cuttings in early autumn.

SIZE: 2.5 x 2.5m (8 x 8ft) after 10 years, ultimately 6m (20ft) tall.

SIGNIFICANT PROBLEMS
Red spider mite on wall-trained plants, scale insects.

Recommended Varieties
The true species is the most frequently seen although there some named forms; 'Sun King' (also called 'Hilsop') is a hardy form that flowers in late winter or early spring, 3 x 3m (10 x 10ft) and has been promoted recently.

Quercus ilex

Trachycarpus fortunei (syn. *Chamaerops excelsa*) AGM
Chusan fan, Windmill palm

FLOWERING or FRUITING
INTEREST: Dense sprays of small
yellow flowers appear in early summer.
Small blue-black fruits are likely only
in the mildest areas.

FOLIAGE INTEREST: Large fan-
shaped leaves of mid-green, up to
1.2m (4ft) wide.

SUITABILITY AS HEDGING: None.

SITE AND SOIL: Full sun and a sheltered position in any well drained soil.
Not suitable for colder gardens in Britain
where it may survive but will always look
brown and ragged.

HARDINESS: Barely hardy to fairly
hardy; the only really hardy palm in
Britain.

SPECIAL CARE: Protect with a deep
bark or bracken mulch and fleece for
the first three years. No pruning necessary. To propagate, remove basal suckers
with two leaves in mid spring and pot up.
Grow on in a greenhouse for a year
before hardening off and planting out.

SIZE: 1 x 1m (3 x 3ft) after five years,
ultimately 4m (13ft) plus.

SIGNIFICANT PROBLEMS
None.

> **Recommended Varieties**
> The true species is the only form
> available.

Trachycarpus fortunei

INDEX

Page numbers in *italics* refer to illustrations.

Abies 72
A. balsamea f. *hudsonia* 72
A. koreana 72
  'Silberlocke' 7, *72, 72*
A. nordmanniana 72, 80
A. procera 72
Acacia dealbata 14, *14*
Alexandrian laurel see *Danae racemosa*
Andromeda polifolia 14-15
  'Alba' *14, 15*
  'Compacta' 15
  'Macrophylla' 15
Araucaria araucana 73, *73*
Arbutus 86
A. x *andrachnoides* 86, *86*
A. unedo 86
A. u. rubra 86
Arctostaphylos uva-ursi 15
  'Vancouver Jade' 15, *15*
Aucuba japonica 16
  'Golden King' 16
  'Longifolia' 16, *16*
  'Salicifolia' 16
  'Variegata' 16
Award of Garden Merit (AGM) 5

Barberry see *Berberis*
Bay laurel see *Laurus nobilis*
Berberis 16
B. buxifolia 'Pygmaea' 17
B. darwinii 17
B. x *frikarti* 'Amstelveen' 17
B. gagnepainii var. *lanceifolia* 17
B. julianae 17
B. linearifolia 'Orange King' 17
B. x *lologensis* 'Apricot Queen' 17
B. x *stenophylla* 17
  'Claret Cascade' *16*
  'Corallina Compacta' 17
B. x *verruculosa* 17
Blue heather see *Phyllodoce empetriformis*
Bog rosemary see *Andromeda polifolia*
Bottle brush see *Callistemon citrinus*
Box see *Buxus sempervirens*
Box-leaved honeysuckle see *Lonicera nitida*
Brachyglottis 17
  'Moira Reid' 17
  'Sunshine' 17

B. monroi 17, *17*
bulbs 10
Bull bay see *Magnolia grandiflora*
Butcher's broom see *Ruscus aculeatus*
Buxus microphylla 'Faulkner' 18
B. sempervirens 18
  'Aureovariegata' 18, *18*
  'Elegantissima' 18
  'Marginata' 18
  'Suffruticosa' 18

Californian lilac see *Ceanothus*
Callistemon citrinus 18-19
  'Splendens' *18*, 19
Calluna vulgaris 19
  'Annemarie' 19
  'Beoley Gold' 19
  'County Wicklow' 19
  'Gold Haze' 19
  'H.E. Beale' 19
  'Kinlochruel' 19
  'Peter Sparkes' 19
  'Robert Chapman' 19
  'Sir John Charrington' 19
  'Sunset' 19
  'Wickwar Flame' 19, *19*
Calocedrus decurrens 73, *73*
Camellia 20-21
  'Cornish Snow' *20*, 21
  'Inspiration' 21
  'Leonard Messel' 21
C. japonica 20, 21
  'Adolphe Audusson' *20*, 21
  'Elegans' 21
  'Jupiter' 21
C. saluenensis 20
C. x *williamsii* 21
  'Anticipation' 21
  'Debbie' *20*, 21
  'Donation' 21
  'Jury's Yellow' 21
  'Saint Ewe' 21
Carpenteria californica 21, *21*
Cassiope 22
  'Edinburgh' 22
  'Randle Cooke' 22, *22*
C. lycopodioides 22
  'Beatrice Lilley' 22
Castor oil plant see *Fatsia japonica*
Ceanothus 22-23
  'Autumnal Blue' 23
  'Blue Mound' 23
  'Burkwoodii' 23
  'Cascade' 23
  'Concha' 23

  'Cynthia Postan' 23
  'Italian Skies' 23
  'Southmead' 23
C. arboreus 'Trewithen Blue' 23, *23*
C. impressus 23
C. prostratus 'Puget Blue' *22*, 23
C. thyrsiflorus repens 23
Cedrus 74
C. deodara 74
C. libani ssp. *atlantica* 74
  Glauca Group 74
  'Glauca Pendula' *74, 74*
C. libani ssp. *libani* 74
Chamaecyparis 75
C. lawsoniana 75
  'Chilworth Silver' 75
  'Columnaris' 75
  'Ellwoodii' 75
  'Ellwood's Gold' 75
  'Minima Aurea' 75
  'Minima Glauca' 75
  'Penbury Blue' 75, *75*
  'Pygmaea Argentea' 75
C. nootkatensis 'Pendula' 75
C. obtusa
  'Crippsii' 75
  'Nana Gracilis' 75
C. pisifera
  'Boulevard' 75
  'Filfera Aurea' 75
C. thyoides 'Ericoides' 75
Chamaerops excelsa see *Trachycarpus fortunei*
Cherry laurel see *Prunus laurocerasus*
Chilean fire bush see *Embothrium coccineum*
Choisya 'Aztec Pearl' 24, *24*
C. ternata 24
  'Sundance' *24*
Chusan fan see *Trachycarpus fortunei*
Cistus 24-25, 43
  'Peggy Sammons' *24*, 25
  'Silver pink' 25
C. x *aguilarii* 'Maculatus' 25
C. x *cyprius* 25
C. x *dansereaui* 'Decumbens' 25
C. formosus see *Halimium lasianthum*
C. x *hybridus* 25
C. ladanifer 25
C. lasianthus see *Halimium lasianthum*
C. x *purpureus* 25

C. x *skanbergii* 25
compost 12
cones 6
conifers 6-7, 11
containers 8
Convolvulus cneorum 25, *25*
Corokia 26
C. buddlejoides 26, *26*
C. cotoneaster 26
C. x *virgata* 26
Coronilla valentina glauca 26
  'Citrina' 26, *26*
  'Variegata' 26
Cotoneaster 28-29
C. arboreus 'Trewithen Blue' *5*
C. cochleatus 29
C. congestus 28, *28*
  'Nana' 29
C. conspicuus 'Decorus' 29
C. dammeri 4, 29, *29*
C. franchetii 29
C. lacteus 29
C. microphyllus 29
C. salicifolius
  'Exburyensis' 29, *29*
  'Pendulus' 29
  'Rothschildianus' 29
C. x *suecicus* 'Coral Beauty' 29
Crinodendron hookerianum 27
C. patagua 27
Cryptomeria japonica 76
  'Elegans' 76, *76*
x *Cupressocyparis leylandii* 76-77
  'Castlewellan' 76, *77*
  'Robinson's Gold' 76
Cupressus 77
C. macrocarpa 77
  'Goldcrest' 77, *77*
  'Golden Pillar' 77
C. sempervirens 'Stricta' 77
Cyathodes colensoi 30, *30*

Daboecia cantabrica 30, *30*
  alba 30
  'Bicolor' 30
  'Praegerae' 30
Daisy bush see *Olearia*
Danae racemosa 31, *31*
Daphne 32
D. blagayana 32, *32*
D. x *burkwoodii* 32
D. cneorum 32
D. laureola 32
D. mezereum 32
D. odora 32
  'Aureomarginata' 32
D. pontica 32

D. tangutica 32
Desfontainia spinosa 33, *33*
diseases 13
Douglas fir see *Pseudotsuga menziesii*
Drimys winteri 33, *33*

Elaeagnus 36
E. x *ebbingei* 36
  'Coastal Gold' 36
  'Gilt Edge' 36, *36*
E. pungens 36
  'Frederici' 36
  'Maculata' 36
  'Variegata' 36
Embothrium coccineum 86, *87*
  'Norquinco' 86
Erica carnea 34-35
  'Ann Sparkes' 34
  'Foxhollow' 34, *34*
  'King George' 34
  'Myretoun Ruby' 34
  'Pink Spangles' 34
  'Springwood White' 34
  'Vivellii' 34
E. cinerea 34
  'Alba Minor' 34, *35*
  'Eden Valley' 34
  'Pink Ice' 34
E. x *darleyensis* 35
  'Arthur Johnson' 35
  'Furzey' 35
  'Ghost Hills' 35
  'Jack H. Brummage' 35
E. erigena 35
  'Golden Lady' 35
  'W.T. Rackcliff' 35
E. tetralix 'Con Underwood' 35
E. vagans 35
  'Lyonesse' 35
  'Mrs D.F. Maxwell' 35, *35*
Eriobotrya japonica 37, *37*
Escallonia 37
  'Apple Blossom' 37
  'Donard Seedling' 37
  'Edinensis' 37
  'Iveyi' 37
  'Peach Blossom' 37
E. rubra 'Crimson Spire' 37
E. r. var. *macrantha* 37
Eucalyptus 87
E. dalrympleana 87
E. globulus 87
E. gunnii 87
E. ssp. *niphophila* 87
E. pauciflora 87, *87*
Eucryphia 90

E. x *intermedia* 'Rostrevor' 90
E. milliganii 90
E. x *nymansensis* 90
  'Nymansay' 90, *90*
Euonymus 38-39
E. fortunei 38, *39*
  'Emerald Gaiety' *38*, 39
  'Emerald 'n' Gold' 39
  'Harlequin' 39
  'Sunspot' 39
E. japonicus 38, *39*
  'Microphyllus
    Albovariegatus' 39, *39*
  'Microphyllus Pulchellus' 39
  'Ovatus Aureus' 39
evergreen 4-5, 6

Fabiana imbricata 39, *39*
x *Fatshedera lizei* 40, *40*
Fatsia japonica 40
  'Variegata' 40, *40*
fertilisers 13
Firethorn see *Pyracantha*
Forrest, George 20
Fuchsia-flowered gooseberry
  see *Ribes speciosum*

Gaultheria 41
G. cuneata 41
G. mucronata 41
  'Bell's Seedling' 41
  'Crimsonia' 41
  'Pink Pearl' 41
G. procumbens 41
G. shallon 41
G. x *wisleyensis* 'Wisley Pearl'
  41, *41*
Gorse see *Ulex europaeus*
Griselinia littoralis 42
  'Bantry Bay' 42, *42*
  'Variegata' 42
ground-cover shrubs 10
Gum tree see *Eucalyptus*

x *Halimiocistus* 43
x *H. sahucii* 43, *43*
x *H. wintonensis* 43
  'Merrist Wood Cream' 43
Halimium, 'Susan' 43, *43*
H. formosum see *H. lasianthum*
H. lasianthum 43
Heath see *Erica carnea*
Heather see *Calluna vulgaris;*
  Erica carnea
Hebe 44-45
  'Autumn Glory' 44, *44*
  'Caledonia' 44
  'County Park' 44

'Emerald Green' 44
'Great Orme' 44
'Midsummer Beauty' 44
'Mrs Winder' 45
'Nicola's Blush' 45
'Pewter Dome' 45
'Red Edge' 45
'Youngii' 45
H. buxifolia 44
H. cupressoides 'Boughton
  Dome' *10*, 44, *44*
H. x *franciscana*
  'Blue Gem' 44
  'Variegata' 44
H. ochracea 'James Stirling' 45
H. pimeleoides 'Quicksilver' 45
H. pinguifolia 'Pagei' 45, *45*
H. rakaiensis 45, *45*
H. salicifolia 45
H. topiaria 45
H. vernicosa 45
Hemlock see *Tsuga*
Holly see *Ilex*
Holm oak see *Quercus ilex*
Houttuynia cordata 50
Hypericum 46
  'Hidcote' 46
H. aegypticum 46, *46*
H. calycinum 46
H. cerastioides 46

Ilex 88-89
I. x *altaclarensis* 89
  'Golden King' *88*, 89
  'Lawsoniana' *88*, 89
I. aquifolium 89
  'Argentea Marginata
    Pendula' 89
  'Bacciflava' 89
  'Ferox' 89, *89*
  'Ferox Argentea' 89
  'Golden Queen' 89
  'Golden Van Tol' 89
  'Handsworth New Silver'
    89
  'J.C. van Tol' 89
  'Pyramidalis' 89
  'Silver Queen' 89
I. crenata 'Golden Gem' 89
I. x *meservae* 'Blue Angel' 89,
  89
Irish heath see *Daboecia
  cantabrica*
Itea ilicifolia *13*, 46-47, *47*

Japanese azaleas 63
Japanese cedar see *Cryptomeria
  japonica*

Japanese medlar see *Eriobotrya
  japonica*
Jasmine box see *Phillyrea
  angustifolia*
Juniperus 78-79
J. chinensis 78
  'Expansa Variegata' 78, *79*
J. communis
  'Compressa' *6*, 78, *79*
  'Hibernica' 79
  'Repanda' 79
J. horizontalis 78
  'Blue Chip' 79, *79*
J. x *pfitzeriana* 'Old Gold' 79
J. sabina 'Tamariscifolia' 79
J. squamata
  'Blue Carpet' 79
  'Blue Star' 79
J. virginiana 'Sulphur
  Spray' 79

Kalmia 47
K. angustifolia 47
K. a. rubra 47
K. latifolia 47, *47*
  'Ostbo Red' 47

Lantern tree see *Crinodendron
  hookerianum*
larch 6
Laurus nobilis *5*, 48, *48*
  'Aurea' 48
Lavandula angustifolia 48-49
  'Hidcote' 49
  'Imperial Gem' 49, *49*
  'Loddon Pink' 49
  'Nana Alba' 49
L. x *intermedia* 'Grappenhall'
  49
L. stoechas 49
Lavender see *Lavandula
  angustifolia*
Leptospermum 49
L. rupestre 49
L. scoparium 49
  'Kiwi' 49, *49*
  'Red Damask' 49
Leucothoe 50
L. axillaris 'Scarletta' 50, *50*
L. walteri 50
  'Rainbow' 50
Leyland cypress see x
  Cupressocyparis leylandii
Ligustrum 50-51
L. lucidum 51
L. ovalifolium 51
  'Aureum' 50, 51
Lonicera fragrantissima 51, *51*

L. nitida 'Baggesen's Gold' 51
L. pileata 51
Loquat see *Eriobotrya japonica*

Magnolia grandiflora 91
  'Exmouth' 91
  'Goliath' 91, *91*
Mahonia 52-53
M. aquifolium 52, 53
  'Apollo' *52*, 53
M. japonica 53
  Bealei Group 53
M. x *media* 53
  'Charity' 53
  'Faith' 53
  'Hope' 53
  'Lionel Fortescue' *52*, 53
Mexican orange blossom see
  Choisya ternata
mixed borders 10
Monkey puzzle see *Araucaria
  araucana*
Mountain heather see
  Phyllodoce empetriformis
moving evergreens 12
Myrtle see *Myrtus communis*
Myrtus communis 53
M. c. tarentina 53, *53*

Nothofagus 91
N. antarctica 91
N. betuloides 91, *91*
Nymans 90
Olearia 54
O. macrodonta 54
O. nummularifolia 54, *54*
O. solandri 54
Osmanthus 54-55
O. x *burkwoodii* 55, *55*
O. delavayi 55
O. heterophyllus 55
  'Goshiki' 55
  'Variegatus' 55
Ozothamnus 55
O. ledifolius 55
O. rosmarinifolius 55
  'Silver Jubilee' 55, *55*

Pachysandra terminalis 56, *56*
  'Variegata' 56
Periwinkle see *Vinca*
pesticides 13
pests 13
Phillyrea angustifolia 56, *56*
Photinia 57
  'Redstart' 57
P. davidiana 57
  'Palette' 57

P. x *fraseri* 'Red Robin' 57,
  57
Phyllodoce empetriformis 57
Picea 80-81
P. abies 80
  'Nidiformis' 81
P. breweriana 81
P. glauca albertiana 'Conica'
  11, *80*, 81
P. mariana 'Nana' 81
P. omorika 81
  'Nana' 81
P. orientalis 'Aurea' 81
P. pungens
  'Hoopsii' 81
  'Koster' 81
P. sitchensis 80
Pieris 58
  'Flaming Silver' 58
  'Forest Flame' 58
P. formosa var. *forrestii*
  'Wakehurst' 58, *58*
P. japonica
  'Little Heath' 58, *58*
  'Mountain Fire' 58
Pine see *Pinus*
Pinus 82-83
P. contorta 82
P. heldreichii var. *leucodermis*
  'Compact Gem' 82
P. montezumae 82, *82*
P. mugo 'Mops' 82
P. m. var. *pumilio* 82
P. nigra 82
P. parviflora 'Adcock's Dwarf'
  82
P. radiata 82
P. strobus 'Radiata' 82
P. sylvestris 82-83
  'Aurea' 83
  'Fastigiata' 83
  'Watereri' 83
P. wallichiana 83, *83*
Pittosporum, 'Garnetti' 59,
  59
P. tenuifolium 58-59
  'Silver Queen' 59
  'Tom Thumb' 59
P. tobira 59
planting 12
Polygala chamaebuxus 59
P. c. var. *grandiflora* 59,
  59
Privet see *Ligustrum*
Prunus laurocerasus 60
  'Otto Luyken' 60, *60*
Pseudotsuga menziesii 83
  'Glauca Pendula' 83, *83*

INDEX

Pyracantha 60-61
  'Orange Charmer' 61
  'Orange Glow' 61, 61
  'Soleil d'Or' 61
  'Teton' 61
P. coccinea 'Red Column'
  61, 61

Quercus ilex 92, 92
Red bearberry see
  Arctostaphylos uva-ursi
Rhamnus alaternus
  'Argenteovariegata' 61,
  61
Rhododendron 62-63
  'Addy Wery' 63
  Blue Tit Group 63
  Bow Bells Group 63
  'Britannia' 12, 62, 63
  'Chikor' 63
  'Dora Amateis' 63
  Elizabeth Group 63
  'Hinomayo' 8, 63, 63
  'Pink Pearl' 63
  'Vuyk's Scarlet' 63
R. campylocarpum 62, 63
R. impeditum 63
R. pemakoense 63
R. ponticum 62, 63
R. sinogrande 62

R. yakushimanum 63
Ribes speciosum 64, 64
Rock rose see Cistus
Rosemary see Rosmarinus
  officinalis
Rosmarinus officinalis 64-65
  'Majorca Pink' 65, 65
  'Miss Jessopp's Upright' 64,
  65
  'Prostratus Group' 65
  'Severn Sea' 65
Rubus tricolor 65, 65
Rue see Ruta graveolens
Ruscus aculeatus 66, 66
R. racemosus see Danae
  racemosa
Ruta graveolens 66
  'Jackman's Blue' 9, 66, 66

Santolina 67
S. chamaecyparissus 67
  'Lambrook Silver' 67, 67
S. pinnata ssp. neapolitana
  'Edward Bowles' 67
Senecio see Brachyglottis
shrubberies 11
Shrubby ragwort see
  Brachyglottis
Shrubby veronica see Hebe
Silver fir see Abies

Silver wattle see Acacia
  dealbata
Skimmia 67
S. x confusa 'Kew Green' 67
S. japonica 67
  'Nymans' 67
  reevesiana 67
  'Rubella' 67
Sophora microphylla 92, 92
  'Sun King' 92
Southern beech see
  Nothofagus
Southern magnolia see
  Magnolia grandiflora
St Dabeoc's heath see
  Daboecia cantabrica
St John's wort see Hypericum
Strawberry tree see Arbutus
Sun rose see Cistus
Sweet bay see Laurus nobilis
Sweetspire see Itea ilicifolia

Taxus baccata 84
  'Fastigiata' 84
  'Repandens' 84
  'Standishii' 7, 84, 84
  'Summergold' 84
  see also yew
Tea tree see Leptospermum
Thuja 84-85

T. occidentalis
  'Danica' 85
  'Holmstrup' 85
  'Rheingold' 85
T. orientalis
  'Aurea Nana' 85
  'Rosedalis' 85
T. plicata 85, 85
  'Rogersii' 85
  'Stoneham Gold' 85
  'Zebrina' 85
Trachycarpus fortunei 93, 93
trees 11
Tricuspidaria lanceolata see
  Crinodendron hookerianum
True cedars see Cedrus
Tsuga 85
T. canadensis 'Jeddeloh' 85
T. heterophylla 85, 85

Ulex europaeus 68
  'Flore Pleno' 68, 68

Vaccinium 69
V. nummularia 69, 69
V. vitis-idaea 69
variegated evergreens 10
Viburnum 70
V. x burkwoodii 70, 70
V. davidii 70

V. rhytidophyllum 70
V. tinus 70, 70
  'Eve Price' 70
  'Gwenllian' 70
  'Lucidum' 70
  'Purpureum' 70
  'Variegatum' 70
Vinca 71
V. major 71
  'Maculata' 71
  'Variegata' 71, 71
V. minor 71
  f. alba 71, 71
  'Argenteovariegata' 71, 71
  'Azurea Flore Pleno' 71, 71

water 12
water loss 7
Williams, J.C. 20
Windmill palm see
  Trachycarpus fortunei
Winter's bark see Drimys
  winteri

yew 6, 11
  see also Taxus baccata

PHOTOGRAPHIC ACKNOWLEDGMENTS

A-Z Botanical Collection/W.Broadhurst 77 left, /Terence Exley 81 left
Eric Crichton 14 Bottom, 16 right, 35 right, 51 Bottom, 58 left, 59 right, 63, 73
left, 76, 81 right
Garden Picture Library/Mark Bolton 55 Bottom, /Brian Carter 49 left,
62 right, /Joan Dear 90, /Ron Evans 87 Top, /John Glover 49 right,
/Neil Holmes 22 right, /Lamontagne 71 Top,
/Steven Wooster 20 Bottom Right
John Glover 20 left, 24 right, 26 Bottom
Andrew Lawson 33 Top, 62 left, 71 Bottom Right, 74, 80
Octopus Publishing Group Ltd. 27, /Neil Holmes 67 left, /Andrew Lawson
Front Cover background, Front Cover bottom right, 1, 30 Bottom, 47 Bottom,
/Howard Rice Front Cover bottom left, Back Cover, 2, 2-3 Background, 4, 5 right,
7 left, 7 right, 8, 9, 10, 11, 12, 14 Top, 15, 17, 18 left, 19, 25, 28, 29 Top, 29
Bottom, 30 Top, 31, 33 Bottom, 34, 36, 37, 38, 39 Top, 39 Bottom, 40 Top, 41,
42, 43 Top, 44 Bottom, 45 left, 45 right, 48, 50, 51 Top, 52 right, 53, 55 Top, 56
Top, 56 Bottom, 57, 58 right, 59 left, 60, 61 Top Right, 61 Bottom, 65 Bottom, 66
left, 66 right, 67 right, 70 left, 70 right, 71 Bottom Left, 72, 73 right, 75, 77 right,

79 left, 82, 84, 85 left, 86, 87 Bottom, 88 left, 88 right, 89 left, 92 Top, 92
Bottom, 93
Photos Horticultural 16 left, 22 left, 26 Top, 35 left, 44 Top, 54, 61 Top Left,
69, 83 right, 89 right
Howard Rice 5 left, 6, 13, 18 right, 20 Top Right, 21, 23, 24 left, 32, 40 Bottom,
47 Top, 52 left, 64, 71 Bottom Centre, 83 left, 91 Top
Eric Sawford 43 Bottom
Harry Smith Collection 46, 65 Top, 68, 78, 79 right, 85 right, 91 Bottom
With thanks to the following, who allowed their gardens and plants to be
photographed:
Ansell's Garden Centre, Horningsea; Ayletts Garden Centre, St Albans;
Cambridge University Botanic Garden; Dr Ruth Chippindale; Docwra's Manor;
East Bergholt Place, Suffolk; Sally Edwards; Holkham Nursery, Norfolk; Madingley
Hall, Cambridge; Royal Horticultural Society's Garden, Wisley, Surrey; Robinson
College, Cambridge; Savill Garden, Surrey; Scotsdale Garden Centre, Great
Shelford; Vision Science Park, Histon, Cambridge;